St. Kilda: A Voyage to the Edge of the World

photo: Cherry Kearton

A ST. KILDAN FOWLER CARRYING A FULMAR.

St Kilda

A Voyage to the Edge of the World

By W. R. Mitchell

for RON HARDIE

(my first guide to the natural wonders of Hirta)

Finlay MacQueen outside his house.

ISBN 1 899863 56 7
First Published 1990
Printed by Lamberts Print & Design, Settle
for
House of Lochar, Isle of Colonsay, Argyll PA61 7YR
1999

Contents

Finlay Gillies

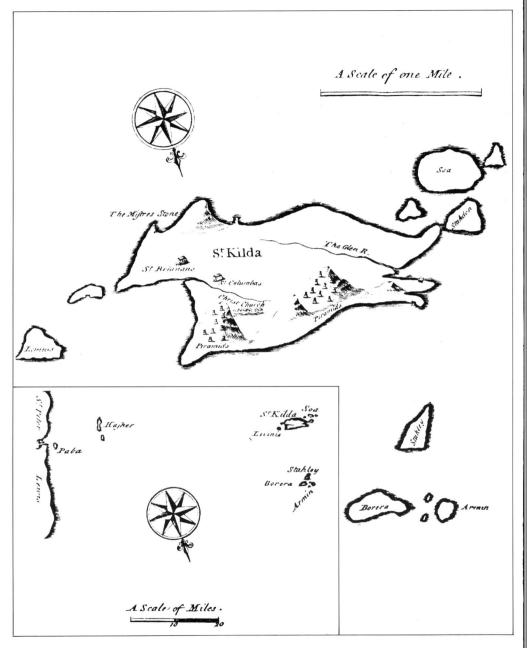

MAP IN MARTIN MARTIN'S ACCOUNT OF ST. KILDA, 1698.

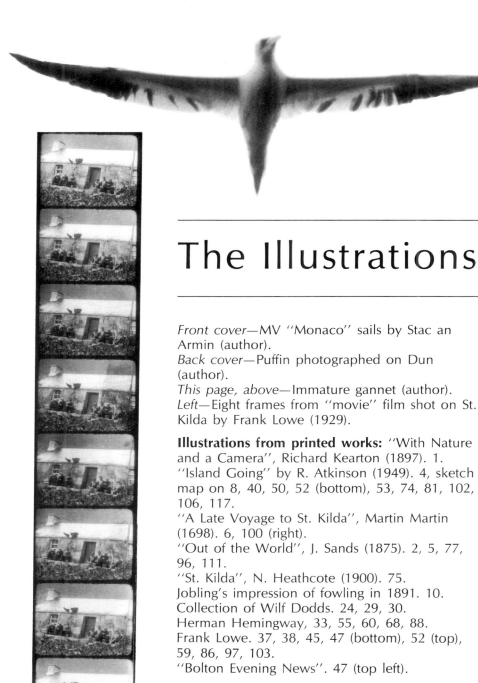

The Illustrations

Front cover—MV "Monaco" sails by Stac an Armin (author).
Back cover—Puffin photographed on Dun (author).
This page, above—Immature gannet (author).
Left—Eight frames from "movie" film shot on St. Kilda by Frank Lowe (1929).

Illustrations from printed works: "With Nature and a Camera", Richard Kearton (1897). 1.
"Island Going" by R. Atkinson (1949). 4, sketch map on 8, 40, 50, 52 (bottom), 53, 74, 81, 102, 106, 117.
"A Late Voyage to St. Kilda", Martin Martin (1698). 6, 100 (right).
"Out of the World", J. Sands (1875). 2, 5, 77, 96, 111.
"St. Kilda", N. Heathcote (1900). 75.
Jobling's impression of fowling in 1891. 10.
Collection of Wilf Dodds. 24, 29, 30.
Herman Hemingway, 33, 55, 60, 68, 88.
Frank Lowe. 37, 38, 45, 47 (bottom), 52 (top), 59, 86, 97, 103.
"Bolton Evening News". 47 (top left).

Other illustrations by the author.

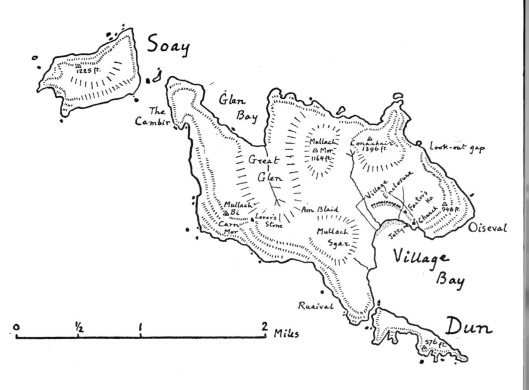

SKETCH MAP OF HIRTA,
SOAY AND DUN.

A Foreword
by the Chairman of
the St. Kilda Club Committee

BILL MITCHELL must be a man with extraordinary patience. To have developed a fascination for St. Kilda in childhood and researched and developed his ambition to visit for some five decades before finally attaining his "Ultima Thule" provides the testimony to his patience.

I have enjoyed being transported from wintry Perthshire to the lush early summer fragrances of Dun with its thousands of whirring puffins and wheeling black-backs, and "seeing" again the sun rise over Boreray and its Stacs.

This book has captured St. Kilda as it is today—the camaraderie of National Trust work parties bent on the maintenance and restoration of the fabric of St. Kildan life combined with the current roles of the Army and Nature Conservancy Council. This is skilfully interwoven with an historical view of St. Kilda and its inhabitants drawn from the prose of centuries but including, for the first time, some anecdotal reminiscences of the Fleetwood trawlermen and their families who played such a major part in the island's communications system at the turn of the century.

St. Kilda, the home of my ancestors, is a "magic" place. This book, like others before, will inspire many to visit and add to the 1,000-1,500 visitors each year who have made the effort in order to attain one goal or another. In the sixtieth year since the evacuation of St. Kilda, my plea is simple—that as far as possible the islands should be preserved as they were known to the St. Kildans and not as we, from another time and place, think they should be preserved.

Alisdair Fleming

A VISITOR'S IMPRESSION OF FOWLING IN 1891

The Rev. Neil Mackenzie wrote of the St. Kildan's efforts during the fulmar harvest: "All this time there is nothing but birds, fat, and feathers everywhere. Their clothes are literally soaked in oil and everywhere inside and outside their houses nothing but feathers; often it looks as if it were snowing."

What a wonderful and strange
experience it all was . . .

*—member of a National Trust
for Scotland working party, 1989.*

The inhabitants live together in a small village carrying all the Signs of an
Extreme Poverty; the Houses are of a low Form, and the Doors all to the
North-East, to secure them from the Shocks of the tempestuous South-
West Winds.

Martin Martin (1698)

The exercise they affect most is climbing of steep rocks. He is the prettiest
man who ventures upon the most inaccessible, though all they gain is the
eggs of the fowls, and the honour to dye, as many of their ancestors, by
breaking their necks.

Sir George MacKenzie of Tarbat (1675)

What has passed of this winter has been rather stormy. All kinds of fowls
that come hither to breed are gone, long ago, to their winter quarters . . .
The people have never been worse off for fuel. Last year was not good
but this one turns out a third less. "Lord, Have mercy on us."

Rev. Neil MacKenzie (Minister, 1830-1844)

They say in the papers that my kinsfolk are now starving, and terribly lonely, and longing and praying to the Socialist Government to be deported—
to some Lowland paradise, I suppose? Nonsense! Food is plentiful now as
it ever was . . . The birds of the rocks and the sheep of the hills are as
numerous as ever . . .

Letter in "The Oban Times", June 2, 1930

THE HANDSOME FACADE OF THE "OBAN TIMES" BUILDING.

A MacBrayne vessel leaves Oban.

In the Beginning

HOWARD BENNETT, proprietor of *The Oban Times,* invited me to spend a day or two in Argyll, using a furnished flat in the pink granite building overlooking Oban Bay. Feeling jaded, I went there in November, confident that western Scotland would provide the necessary pick-me-up: a remedy compounded of fresh air and exercise in a setting of burns and bens.

Alas, the precious sunshine was intercepted by rain-bearing cloud that stretched from Ben Cruachan to the islands. A succession of "wee showers" kept the streets awash and beat the sea into submission, leaving it listless and dull grey like old pewter.

So I created a cosy environment within the flat, using an electric fire and some standard lamps with rosy shades. The early morning ritual included a soak in hot water. It pleased me to think that a large bath in the spacious bathroom had been used by a succession of red-haired Editors of *The Oban Times.* In a fanciful moment I pictured them, relaxed and happy in a soapy swell, composing next week's editorials and in pleasant anticipation of a wee drammie.

I used the bath therapeutically, to get the chill from my joints.

Who needed television when I could look out on to an incessant movement of people, vehicles and boats? In between rain showers, the last few indomitable tourists of the year were being persuaded to make boat trips unaware that outside the calm Bay lay the broad corrugations of a fearsome ocean.

On my second evening I made a discovery that transformed my Highland holiday. It also led to the writing of (yet another) book about St. Kilda, the spectacular group of islands and stacks, remnants of an ancient volcano, jutting from the Atlantic Ocean on the Sunset Coast of Scotland.

My discovery was a newspaper file—copies of *The Oban Times* for the year 1930. As I turned the yellowing pages, I saw frequent references to St. Kilda, and more precisely to the story of the last days of a remote, proud and self-reliant community who were evacuated to the mainland on Friday, August 29, 1930.

I was already suffering from St. Kilditis, an incurable disease. I became infected as a small boy, when I read a book by the Kearton brothers, Richard and Cherry, pioneer wildlife photographers, who landed on St. Kilda in 1898 and wrote graphically about it.

I read every book that came my way about the islands "at the edge of the world." In the summer of 1988, I observed St. Kilda from the air during a flight from Reykjavik in Iceland to Glasgow. Having had breakfast, I leaned back in my chair to recall some of the Icelandic experiences. Soon afterwards, the pilot of the aircraft mentioned that St. Kilda was in view, to starboard, and so it was—a scattering of green-topped islets and white-topped stacks with an Omo-white frill of foam as the ocean smacked its lips against the smooth volcanic rocks.

Once, on Harris, at a village shop that had just acquired a new front door—that of a redundant telephone box, guaranteed to withstand a Hebridean gale—I expressed interest in St. Kilda, which lies within the parish of Harris. The shopkeeper took me outdoors and pointed out a blue smudge on the horizon. "That," he said, "is St. Kilda." Discovering more about that smudge, from personal experience, thereafter became an obsession.

I wanted to stand on the highest sea cliff in Britain—to look down on ledges full of croaking fulmars and across to the highest sea-stacks in Britain. It became a major ambition to watch puffins return to the lichened rocks of Dun (pronounced Doon) with beaks full of tiny fish for their young. I longed to hear the voices of several million seabirds resounding in the echo-chambers between the cliff faces. There would be the growling of gannets and guillemots and the yelping of the great skua, which is known in northern Scotland as the bonxie.

St. Kilda is well suited to the needs of birds that spend most of the year on the ocean, its islets and stacks being free of land-based predators like rats. The humans who preyed on birds and their eggs were careful not to do this to excess. What food the St Kildans did not consume while fresh, they stored—along with hay, peat, even clothes—in drystone structures known as cleits (the purist uses the plural *cleitean*), over 1,200 of which have been recorded on Hirta alone.

At St Kilda, pieces of land, vestiges of the Big (volcanic) Bang, are scattered over the sea. Hirta, the main island, has three satellites—Soay, Dun and Levenish. Some four miles from Hirta lies Boreray, presiding over two immense stacks which in spring and summer are white with the recumbent forms of gannets at the largest of the world's gannetries.

These thoughts, and many more, came to mind during that autumnal holiday at Oban. As I turned the yellowing pages of the newspaper file for 1930, I began to entertain the idea of actually going to St Kilda. Mentioning my ambition to a fisherman I met on the Railway Quay at Oban, I heard him say: "You want to leave St Kilda alone at this time of year..."

Back at the flat, my eyes prickled with fatigue as I read the columns of type relating to St Kilda. The journalists of the time had been provided with many "human interest" stories. On February 22, 1930, the fishery cruiser *Norna* reached St Kilda after sailing from Leith via the Pentland Firth, and a sick woman was removed to Glasgow. It was the second attempt of Dr Shearer, Department of Health for Scotland, to reach the lonely islands. The cruiser collected him at Loch Tarbert, Harris.

Outside influences, including tourism, were already destroying the self-reliance of the St Kildans. The visitors had tales to tell of foul weather and close encounters with watery graves. On August 30, the *Hebrides* had a calm passage to St Kilda, and in Village Bay [referred to in the account as Parson's Bay] the islanders came out in their boats to collect the passengers and take them ashore for a short time.

"The wind began to freshen and Captain John MacKinnon, who had many experiences of St Kildan storms, at once blew the steamer's whistle for the return of those who had landed. The natives then set off to take the passengers back to the steamer, but the waves were rising. Parson's Bay is no match for the whole force of the Mighty Atlantic, and the St Kildan boat was dashed against the pier, holed and sank.

"The situation became tense. The natives naturally would not risk their other boat. The visitors were faced with an unprepared stay on the island. But by means of signalling to the *Hebrides,* one of her boats was lowered, manned and brought to the landing stage. It was not without danger and only by good seamanship were the passengers taken off and received on board..."

The Evacuation of St. Kilda is a heart-stirring story in itself, as I discovered on those long November evenings in the flat overlooking Oban Bay. Almost at the end of the year 1930, the newspaper reported on the fate of "the St. Kilda relics"—the communion vessels, linens and tokens. It seems that the Highlands and Islands Committee of the Church of Scotland decided they would be housed in the Church's museum at the Tolbooth, Castlehill, Edinburgh.

Back at home, I re-read the 1896 account of how the Kearton brothers, sons of a Pennine gamekeeper, sailed to St. Kilda. They had left their native Swaledale for jobs with Cassells, the publishers, in London, and began to write their natural history books at a time when they could take advantage of the new half-tone system of block-making, which had just been introduced from America.

A love of wild birds and photography led them to visit most of the great seabird nesting areas of Britain and Ireland. As they made arrangements to visit St. Kilda, they described it as "the paradise of British ornithologists". The adventure began as they sailed from the Clyde in the *Dunara Castle*.

The mate from a Fleetwood trawler anchored in Village Bay, in the period of the 1930s when Hirta had no human inhabitants, admires two newly-born lambs of the Soay breed.

Two young men who had grown up among the unsophisticated dalesfolk of north-west Yorkshire got on well with the St. Kildans and were able to photograph them at home and during the fowling expeditions.

Their narrative became a worthy addition to the growing number of books dealing with first-hand experience on the Hebridean outliers.

The voyage to St. Kilda may still be fraught with difficulty. The sea is stirred up by wind and wave. Winter gales can be unbelievably violent, as I was to hear from a man who experienced one with a wind speed gusting at 195 miles an hour.

The steamer on which the Keartons sailed took to rolling and pitching in a disconcerting way. On the return journey, in wild weather, the boat hit a rock. Richard Kearton, fearing that it would sink, dived below for his box of St. Kilda negatives, determined that he and they would survive.

For 50 years, I kept St. Kilda at the back of my mind as a special place to be visited when I retired from work and I need not worry about St. Kilda's climatic tantrums. What matter if I had to wait a week to get there and a fortnight before I could return?

Now *The Oban Times* reminded me of my dreams.

The newspaper file also reminded me of chats I had with Betty and Frank Lowe, of Bolton, who visited St. Kilda on their honeymoon in 1929. Frank, like me and many others, had been inspired by the work of the Keartons. I have Frank's camera, his photographic plates and notes about the fortnight's expedition in 1929, which was by trawler from Stornoway. In the following year, St. Kilda was evacuated, so they were among the last to observe an ancient way of life.

Incidentally, Frank and Betty died within a short time of each other, while visiting their daughter Anne in Canada. Anne subsequently visited Bolton to settle up her parents' affairs. She handed me a plastic bag. "I think father would have liked you to have these." Inside were two souvenirs of St. Kilda, collected in 1929, one being an ingenious wooden door-lock and the other a bird snare.

Hearing that Fleetwood trawlers often sheltered in the lee of St. Kilda during gales, and that some skippers collected or delivered mail, I went to the Lancashire seaside town and interviewed men and women who remembered the St. Kildan years, when Fleetwood children went on "pleasure trips" on the trawlers during the long summer holiday.

Letters I received from Marsaili MacKinnon following an inquiry about St. Kilda that was published in *The Oban Times* told me not only about the St. Kildans she knew—and the St. Kilda she visited with a working party in

1970—but about the fishermen's contribution to the well-being of the islanders.

I told Mrs MacKinnon about my proposed book; she wrote: "I am partticularly pleased that you are including stories from the trawlermen of Fleetwood. I have long felt that they, like their brethren from Grimsby, Hull, North Shields, Aberdeen and Fraserburgh, have never been given their due place and credit on the story of St. Kilda pre-1930. . .

"They were a lifeline to the islanders—for food in times of scarcity, for medicines and other necessities, for getting mail in and out, for getting to the mainland to visit relatives and getting ill people to hospital on the mainland (not to mention for keeping old Finlay MacQueen supplied with tobacco!). I remember Lachie Macdonald saying that they were the true friends of the St. Kildans."

Enclosed with the letters was a newpaper cutting, prefaced by the words "Airlift St. Kilda", in which it was related that an injured fisherman from the Aberdeen trawler *Marlewood* had been airlifted to hospital by the Stornoway Coastguard helicopter on Sunday afternoon after receiving attention from army medics on St. Kilda. A picture showed the patient being lifted off the island by the Bristow rescue helicopter.

The notion of aircraft being able to hover would have been considered fantastic in 1925 when Jack Kelly, a nine-year-old Fleetwood lad, first went to St. Kilda. "I had a few sweets and apples that my mother had put in my seabag. I gave them to the children on the island. Treats like that were rare for them and they were thrilled." Jack recalled that the island lads wore woollen jerseys and scarves, rough trousers and boots made from sealskin.

He saw the white-bearded elders, including Finlay MacQueen, then the leader of the little community. Finlay spoke softly, in Gaelic. The Fleetwood men left gifts in the form of coal, fish, flour and other foodstuffs.

Jack was to return to St. Kilda as a trawlerman and eventually as a skipper. He showed me colour film he had "shot" of trawlers in mountainous seas off Hirta. "It was an awe-inspiring spot, and not only for the tumult of a gale. I've been on my own in the wheelhouse many times while fishing off Kilda. On a starry night, I'd think about the Creation—about how such a scene had come to pass. It was that sort of place."

Not everyone shared his enthusiasm. Walter Carter, thoroughly depressed at the thought of another voyage, was seen dragging his kitbag along the road to Fleetwood docks. He told a friend: "Anyone who goes to sea for a living would go to hell for a pastime." His sister, Alice, was only eight years old when she and her brother George joined their father, Skipper Reggie Carter, for a "pleasure trip" to the fishing grounds in the steam trawler *Gladys*.

Father gave up his bunk to his little daughter; he and George slept on the settee in the skipper's diminutive cabin under the wheelhouse. "Every morning when I got up, the crew kept asking me if I felt poorly," Alice recalls. "I didn't realise you were supposed to get seasick—and I wasn't!"

Alice and George, the children of Skipper Reggie Carter, on a Fleetwood trawler heading for the fishing grounds off St. Kilda.

The voyage of the *Gladys* was memorable because the fishermen made the children a hammock from some old netting; the hammock was slung on deck. So they were not "under the feet" of the men as they handled a catch. Alice wore a sou'wester, a small woollen muffler and a black and white check coat with a velvet collar.

She and her brother carried their spare clothing, socks and tooth brushes in a pillow case. "Fortunately, each time I went to sea we had a good cook..." She remembers "lovely roasts of beef and lamb." The trawler put into Village Bay on Hirta because her father was delivering some mail. "He became known in a newspaper article as 'St. Kilda's Guardian Angel'."

Having retired from the Editorship of *The Dalesman* magazine, and being theoretically free to do whatever I wished, I wrote to the National Trust for Scotland, applying to join a St. Kilda working party. My application was successful.

On June 3, 1989, I sailed for the isles of my dreams...

19

A

VOYAGE

TO

St. KILDA.

The remoteſt of all the *Hebrides*, or Weſtern Iſles of *Scotland*:

GIVING

An ACCOUNT of the very remarkable Inhabitants of that Place, their Beauty and ſingular Chaſtity (Fornication and Adultery being unknown among them); their Genius for Poetry, Muſic, Dancing; their ſurpriſing Dexterity in climbing the Rocks, and Walls of Houſes; Diverſions, Habit, Food, Language, Diſeaſes and Methods of Cure; their extenſive Charity; their Contempt of Gold and Silver, as below the Dignity of Human Nature; their Religious Ceremonies, Notion of Spirits and Viſions, *&c. &c.*

To which is added,

An ACCOUNT of *Roderick*, the late Impoſtor there, pretending to be ſent by St. *John Baptiſt* with new Revelations and Diſcoveries; his Diabolical Inventions, Attempts upon the Women, *&c.*

BY M. MARTIN, GENT.
The FOURTH EDITION, correſted.

The Inhabitants of St. Kilda are almoſt the only People in the World who feel the Sweetneſs of true Liberty; what the Condition of the People in the Golden Age is feigned to be, that theirs really is. P. 67.

LONDON:

Printed for DAN. BROWNE, without *Temple-Bar*; and LOCKYER DAVIS, in *Fleet-Street*.
MDCCLIII.

Title page from the fourth edition of Martin Martin's account of his visit to St. Kilda, originally published in 1698.

Outward Bound for Kilda

AS OUR BOAT left sheltered water in the Sound of Harris and became a dot on the North Atlantic, the cutlery began to rattle. We dampened the cloths on the saloon tables for extra adhesion. Cubby MacKinnon, the skipper, directed MV Monaco, this converted Danish fishing boat, due west—to St. Kilda.

Our voyage to "the islands at the edge of the world" was now in its second day. We had cast off from the Railway Quay at Oban and had ridden the flow-tide along the Sound of Mull to the choppy water off Ardnamurchan, the most westerly point on the British mainland. The Sma' Isles—Muck, Eigg, Rum, Canna—lay scattered across a bird busy sea. To the west, Barra Head heralded the appearances of The Western Isles.

I felt in a romantic mood and chanted:

> From the lone shieling and the misty island
> Mountains divide as and a waste of sea;
> Yet still our hearts are true, our hearts are Highland.
> And we in dreams behold the Hebrides.

In June, the Hebridean night is just a blink between two long days. We spent an hour or two of darkness tied up at Lochmaddy, sharing a jetty with a MacBrayne car ferry, which blazed with light. The engine of the Monaco was re-started at 5am, which was somewhat later than the skipper had intended. Snugly cocooned in my sleeping bag, I heard the engine beat quicken. The Monaco swayed slightly. We were awa'. Half dressed, and with the sleep mist still in my eyes, I staggered on to the foredeck, which had such a steep gradient I entertained the thought of using crampons.

MV Monaco, built in Esbjerg, Denmark, in 1970, having oak resting against oak, proved to be ideal for the St. Kilda run.

21

At my appearance on deck the skipper gave a friendly wave. His wife, Kate, described the morning as "right bonnie", which it was—clear, sunlit and so calm that a passing gull might admire its reflection in the sea.

We made up for the delay—it being high water—by using the (buoyed) Cope Channel in the sound of Harris. Arctic terns, on feeding sorties from the islets, jerked their way about the sky; their wings seemed translucent when they were backlit by the sun.

Black guillemots—tysties to the northern Scots—were resting on the buoys, where they either stayed, rocking gently in the wake of the *Monaco,* or they slipped into the water and flew, pattering on red feet, showing off the white patches on their wings. In flight, they appeared to flicker like butterflies.

It was at this moment that Cubby MacKinnon's wife, Kate, said, brightly: "We're going round the corner... wet the cloths!" Whatever had been left on the tables now had fixed positions.

So we left the shelter of the Hebrides, Scotland's mighty natural breakwater. The sea-tone was Prussian blue, frilly white at the edges. The western cliffs provided an unyielding barrier to the Atlantic waves which, forming hundreds of miles away, now exploded in sheets of spray.

The Hebrides remained in sunshine. We passed under the edge of a canopy of cloud that extended to the western horizon. For several hours we headed westwards, at eight or nine knots, with the boat breasting a slight swell. Gannets were in strong, silent flight. A shearwater lived up to its name, dipping low to stroke the waves with its wings. A puffin, with its permanent look of surprise, made frantic efforts to become airborne, paddling with its coral-red feet and working the slender wings so furiously I entertained the idea that one of them might break off through bone-fatigue.

The one member of our party who felt seasick and who had "taken to her bed" re-appeared to view. Relieved that sea conditions were "nae so bad", she plucked the first stray thought from her mind: "A friend tells me it takes two and a-half minutes to boil a puffin egg."

This was proving to be an easy passage. *Monaco* had six cabins, all having hand basins with taps for hot and cold water. In the saloon, the seating was upholstered.

For the first detailed crossing from The Long Island to St. Kilda, in 1697, one Martin Martin was rowed in an open boat for over 40 miles from Harris. He recorded: "Our crew became extremely fatigued and discouraged without the sight of land for sixteen hours." And so they might, for the weather was inclement. One storm sent them scurrying for shelter under the northern cliffs of Boreray. "The storm did almost drive us to the ocean... our men laid aside all hopes of life." Then the weather relented; the sea went calm and the boat was rowed into Village Bay, on the island

22

of Hirta, with dignity.

As related, my interest in St. Kilda was aroused by reading an account left by two Yorkshire Dalesmen—Richard and Cherry Kearton. They were born in Swaledale, about the middle of northern England, where there was not the faintest whiff of a salt breeze. In 1896, when outward bound from the Clyde in the steamer *Dunara Castle* they groaned with anguish as it

Peter Snasdell, of Fleetwood, recalls St. Kilda
from the steam trawler days.

rolled and pitched. Richard noted that "most of her passengers lost all interest in wallowing porpoises and plunging gannets, and experienced those unpleasant sensations which for a time rob all natural objects of their charm."

On my crossing to St. Kilda, I could not believe my good fortune in having calm weather, so fresh in my mind was that film I had seen at Skipper Kelly's home in Fleetwood—of trawlers bucking like bronco's on a gale-lashed sea and the 1,000 ft cliffs of St. Kilda fringed by white water.

"Kildas" lay off the main shipping routes but were familiar to the Lancashiremen. A Fleetwood skipper had a choice of the "inside" or the "outside" route to the fishing grounds, where the special requirement was for hake. Being "inside" meant taking shelter from the Hebrides. The "outside" course lay northwards from Rathlin, off Ireland.

Peter Snasdell, one of the last of the Fleetwood men with memories of fishing from steam trawlers, used to visit St. Kilda and other Hebridean outliers—Sula Sgeir, North Rona and the Flannan Islands. He had trawled off Foula, the westernmost of the Shetland group.

Peter told me that sometimes the men went ashore; they met and befriended local people. Arthur Green, the skipper of a trawler in which Peter sailed in the early 1930s, landed in a small boat on the Flannans to have a chat with a lighthouse keeper he knew well. "The Flannan Islands were cod and haddock. At Sula Sgeir, you could go right in the deep water, like you do at Kildas, and there was hake. At North Rona, there was more hake..."

Peter was but nine years of age when he first saw, over breaking waves, the billowing form of Hirta and the attendant islets of Dun and Soay. The skipper, Peter's Uncle Billy, had sailed with Sydney Arthur Tonner, "the first man to be paid to deliver mail to St. Kilda."

Young Peter's introduction of the remote islands came after the "outside" route had been followed. The skipper spurned the shelter provided by the Hebrides. It called for a high standard of navigation 60 years ago

The Fleetwood steam trawler "Daily Mail".

One of the trawlers in which Peter Snasdell toured the northern seas.

to set a course and maintain it northwards from Rathlin to St. Kilda or to Rockall, a solitary stack at the edge of the Continental Shelf.

"In bad weather, you kept going, with everything battened down. You put your stem to the wind all the time in the worst conditions. That's what you did at St. Kilda when a gale was blowing. I remember being in a 100 mile an hour wind for seven days. It was just life and death. To take shelter from Kilda we would have had to 'run' [to put the sea behind the boat] and that was the most dangerous thing anyone could do."

In 1930, Peter sailed to St. Kilda in a coal-fired trawler skippered by Arthur Green, a Hull man who had graduated from a nautical school and was an expert navigator at a time when nobody could be accurate to within a couple of miles. "There was a sextant, but nobody used it much because you did not often see the sun..."

A typical Fleetwood trawler carried a skipper, mate, bosun, three or four deckhands, wireless operator, chief engineer, a second engineer, two fireman and a cook. The firemen shovelled their way to and from "Kildas", burning 150 tons of coal in the process.

Peter told me that his trip in 1930 took place in August, a stormy time of the year. "The weather was atrocious. St. Kilda is a funny place. The islands breed winds. I've known times when the wind was howling and rain fell like stair-rods. Twenty miles away, the weather was calm and sunny.''

The trawl of those days was made of sizal, with the headline 100 feet long and ''otter doors'' to keep the mouth of the net open. When fishing, a trawlerman was on his feet, soaked by sea spray, for 22 hours a day. ''You caught hake in the daylight, so the fish would be on the bottom from about 9 o'clock in the morning to 4 or 5 o'clock at night. After that, you had finished. If you got out to 300 fathoms, you'd get all sorts of rubbish like rat-fish.''

It was a joyous time if a basking shark was netted. ''They paid you what was called 'liver money'. All the liver out of the fish was saved in barrels. If we got a basking shark, we clapped our hands because it had a big liver. It would fill a 40 gallon drum.''

In the early 1930s, half a dozen French lobster boats, under sail, would be bobbing on the water off St. Kilda. The men laid ''fleets'' of lobster pots around the rocks. ''Those boats drew so little water, they could operate much closer-in than the trawlers. Once, when we were fishing under Boreray, the French boats came alongside and we gave them the fish we did not want—squid and the like. They used it as bait for their lobster pots. We had wireless, using Morse. One day a Frenchman asked us to send a message to his home town in France.''

Off St. Kilda, there were no wrecks to contend with—''just odd patches of boulders. We cleared them up. If we collected a boulder in the trawl we kept in on deck till it was time to go home. Then we'd drop it off Barra Head. Some of those boulders weighed three or four hundredweight!''

My first contact with the Fleetwood fishermen came about after I had been told that they had given fresh white bread to the St. Kildans, to whom it was a great delicacy. In point of fact, there was little spare food on the trawlers but the fishermen were well disposed towards the islanders.

''When you set off from port, you had a 'fry'—one meal of bacon—so that the cook did not need to make another hot meal for a while. The cook would bake some white bread. After that, it was down-to-earth food, with soup, potatoes and vegetables. Towards the end of the trip, you had no vegetables. They'd 'gone off'.''

At times, the trawlermen emulated the St. Kildans and ate some seabirds. Arthur Green, the Skipper, gave a couple of gannets to the cook, who plucked them. Gannets could be either boiled or roasted. ''Seabirds used to follow you; they were perched all over the ship. When we were coming home, there was bird-muck everywhere. We tried to clean it up, but you couldn't get it off.''

A wise skipper kept plenty of water between himself and the isles.

"Two ships were wrecked—lost with all hands. One ship was called *Briarlyn* and the other *Kumu*. They were both Fleetwood boats. The skipper used to say to me: 'If we get a big bag of fish this haul, I'll go and drop the anchor down the *Kumu's* funnel. He was joking with me. But he knew just where the *Kumu* was."

The Fleetwood trawlers did not observe a close season. They sailed to St. Kilda in winter and summer alike. Winter had its pleasant days but was also a time of raw winds and flurries of snow. The days were short and often sunless. The men had to trawl in deep water. "The fish might be 30 or 40 miles off Kildas, towards Rockall. That old rock is only about 75 feet high. It's just stuck up there on its own. They've blasted off the top of the rock and put a beacon on it now."

In the heyday of trawling from Fleetwood, 40 or 50 trawlers at a time bobbed on the water off St. Kilda. Just after the 1939-40 war, men like Peter Snasdell were returning from St. Kilda with up to 1,000 ten-stone boxes of hake. "This was always a priority fish. Manchester used to live off it. London got skate and dogfish."

When the aids to navigation were improved, the trawlermen could shoot their nets west of Barra Head and tow in the same water right round the Hebrides to the Butt of Lewis, on to Foula and, from the 1950s, to Muckle Flugga, Shetland. The Flugga, and the Outstack, are the northernmost rocks in Britain. The fishermen's voyages were all to do with the abundance or scarcity of hake. They looked for a declining number of areas where this fish was still common. Peter Snasdell told me: "Then the herring went. And so did the hake that had fed on them."

Skipper Jim Port, in command of the Fleetwood steam trawler *Julia Brierley,* had a nerve-wracking trip to St. Kilda in November, 1957. He was one of the last of the Lancashiremen to fish off the celebrated islands. His ultimate destination was what was known as the "wall of death", the edge of the Continental Shelf, where the seabed falls away into the Atlantic abyss.

Skipper Port had just arrived on the grounds west of St. Kilda when the weather—and also the health of his bosun—deteriorated. A gale blew up and the trawler had to be kept head to wind. The luckless bosun, Michael Quinn, had an abdominal pain which his Skipper, after consulting a first aid manual, diagnosed as appendicitis.

He recalled for readers of the *Evening Gazette,* in Lancashire: "I was worried about his condition but I knew there was no way we could take him back to civilisation because the weather was so bad we had to stay head to wind and dodge out the storm. To head east would have been very dangerous, too great a risk".

He called Oban radio to discuss the case. The message was picked up by RAF personnel on St. Kilda, where medical help was now available. Nothing could be done until the gale moderated. Every 12 hours, the skipper reported to the RAF on the condition of his bosun. Two days later, as the wind fell away, the trawler entered Village Bay and dropped anchor.

The trawler's lifeboat was launched with five volunteers at the oars; and the bosun was taken ashore. "There was still a big swell running and

Skipper Jack Kelly, of Fleetwood.

it was breaking surf on the beach. I watched them every inch of the way through the binoculars but then I lost them as they got into the surf. Had they overturned? Had they made it? I must have aged 10 years but it was OK." They left the sick man on Hirta.

Happily, the bosun did not have appendicitis; he was given pain-killing drugs and good treatment from the RAF. Twelve days later, he was picked up at St. Kilda by the *Julia Brierley* and taken back to Fleetwood where his medical treatment was continued.

Having enjoyed listening to the veterans of Fleetwood who had first-hand knowledge of fishing off St. Kilda, I was now staring westwards until my eyes prickled with fatigue, anxious to catch the first, exciting view of the islands at the edge of the world.

Monaco had the sea to herself. She proceeded at a steady pace, with a flurry of foam at her bows. I found Cubby joyfully looking over the bows

Fleetwood trawler "Gladys" sheltering in Village Bay, 1930. The photograph was taken from the "Luneda" by Wilf Dodds, using a box camera.

at the bubbling, surging spume. "It gives me the sort of pleasure someone else will get from looking at pictures in a coal fire. . ."

Out here there were no squawking gulls. The true birds of the sea appeared, passed the boat and disappeared with a minimum of wing movement and no sound. Fulmar, petrel, gannet, shearwater, used the "lift" provided by the light wind and the swell. The fulmars that passed near or even over the ship were mute, expressionless. The first fulmar of the day was pink, its normally pale feathers having caught the rays of the newly-risen sun. Fleetwood men call fulmars "mollies".

Skipper Jack Kelly, of Fleetwood, had told me that on his first visit to St. Kilda he was sailing in the *Malaga*, a trawler of about 110 feet which had been built in Canada. It was a boat reduced to bare essentials, from the cramped fo'csle to the little boat hanging from davits at the stern. The *Malaga* had not a single luxurious feature. Jack, then aged 14½ years, asked the bosun, Peter Shard, where they were going. Peter replied: "We're going sou'west o' Kildas."

Young Jack Kelly was fascinated by all he saw as the boat steamed to its required depth of 85 fathoms. "Then we shot the gear and towed up north. When hake fishing, if you towed north rather than south you got more fish. Don't ask me why. We towed one day and most of the next, getting into an area nor'west of St. Kilda."

The fishing was quite good. A full net broke the surface of the sea with the effect of an explosion. "The sea birds, including the mollies were soon there." It was blowing hard. "We ran into Village Bay for shelter. We were in there for two days."

Of the sea birds, Jack retained special memories of the gannets. "You'd be trawling on a nice day, with not a bird in sight—no gannets, no

29

mollies, nothing—and as soon as the steam winch started when the trawl was being brought in, the sky would fill up with birds. Then you'd see the gannets diving. It's amazing how they managed to miss one another, because there were not hundreds—but thousands! Especially at Kildas.

"The gannets took the small fish that got free of the trawl. The mollies waited until you'd started to cut up the fish. When the guts were washed through the scuppers, you'd see a mass of mollies quacking astern."

Fleetwood men fished between the stacks and Boreray. The stacks sprang high from the water and yet the trawler that cruised near them might have 30 fathoms of water beneath its keel. Working close in, when the weather conditions were favourable, Jack drew up some excellent turbot and haddock. "You can fish up to 100 yards from Boreray. We used to get quite big bags of dogfish there."

Skipper Port was to remember the great gannet colony of Boreray, which he first saw as a boy of 14 years. "We'd sound the siren and the birds would fly off the cliffs and darken the sky. It was amazing."

The Fleetwood connection with St. Kilda began about 1924. The last time a Fleetwood vessel went there was about 1970. It was a Glorious Half Century for the fishermen.

FD116 "Swan", fringed with sea-foam, as she sails towards St. Kilda.

Landfall on Hirta

FROM THE FOREDECK of *Monaco*, I beheld the mightly Atlantic. The ocean that has a reputation for its excesses—for gale and seething water—was now in a gentle mood, with no white-tops. As *Monaco* stirred the water, it swirled and bubbled.

I varied the pastime of horizon-watching by making cups of tea for fellow voyagers. I dozed on an improvised seat—three old lorry tyres that buttress the ship's side when in harbour. Someone made tea. There was time for another wee nap, followed by another spell of horizon-watching.

Slowly, the sun-rimmed Hebrides were lost to sight. St. Kilda, cloud-wrapped, came slowly into view. No one could be precise just when Boreray detached itself from the mist, but suddenly there it was—a sea cliff, with no apparent means of support. It might have been propped against the sky. This rock wall, over 1,200 feet high, was impressive even at a range of several miles.

My heart-beat quickened at the prospect of a St. Kildan landfall; the engine beat of MV *Monaco* remained constant as she ploughed on, being overtaken by homing seabirds—by gannets, guillemots, razorbills and puffins. It was comforting to notice that they were taking precisely the same course as the boat.

The indomitable Irish hermits who sailed on grey northern seas, looking for remote and quiet places where they could ponder on Eternity, must have been re-assured by the confident flight of birds. There must be land in prospect! St. Donna founded a monastery on Eigg and St. Flanna gave his name to the Flannan Isles, which jut from an uneasy sea north-west of Gallan Head.

It is more than likely that a hermit or two, those Cockleshell Heroes, settled on the islands of the St. Kilda group. The name St. Kilda may simply be a corruption of the Norse "kelda", meaning a well, from the local pronunciation for "Hirtir", which the Norse settlers bestowed on the principal island of the group. "Hirtir" appears to have been recorded in error as St. Kilda in some Dutch sailing instructions published in 1652. The Dutch were among the first to exploit the Scottish fisheries. The association continues. Even as we sailed to St. Kilda, modern Dutch trawlers were fishing in the area.

During more steady progress, Boreray was joined by other islets. They, too, were like dark grey cut-outs propped against the sky. The mist returned. When it seemed that the world would be plunged into general gloom, the sun found a hole in cloud. Yellow rays, like spotlights at a theatre, revealed limited areas with clarity and colour.

Cubby MacKinnon found conditions were suitable for a cruise near Boreray and its attendant stacks. Boreray had no human residents. In the old days, the St.Kildans visited it to attend to the sheep and for fowling purposes. It must have been a brave sight when men, a few children and some lively dogs landed from open boats on to hard rock to attend to the sheep-clipping.

Boreray had been on my mind since I met Flora, a native of St. Kilda, at her home at Kincardine Bridge. In June, 1922, her father, Donald Gillies,

The gannet-whitened Stacs of Lee and Armin off Boreray.

Nesting gannets. In the 17th century, the St. Kildan fowlers, after a precarious sea crossing, and equally precarious ascent of the Stacs, were catching over 22,000 gannets a year.

aged 36, had been in the party of wool-clippers on Boreray when he was taken ill with appendicitis.

The islanders had their own method of communicating between Boreray and Hirta; they called up the boat by cutting pieces of turf from a prominent grassy slope. So it was when Donald Gillies became ill. His young daughter, Chrissie, was in the party on the island. Those on Hirta who awaited the return of the boat were not to know for some hours who had been afflicted. Nor, indeed, that Donald Gillies had died. His body was reverently (and quietly) borne ashore. A television documentary about St. Kilda gave the impression that at such times, the womenfolk wailed as a noisy expression of their anguish.

Boreray was everything I expected a Hebridean outlier to be. I was thrilled by the sight of upjutting rock, by rows of gannets, by the thousands of circling seabirds and the dull thud of the sea as it expended itself against smooth rock.

The clonk of return-mirrors in reflex cameras joined a variety of natural sounds. A photographer who groaned when her camera "jammed" discovered it was not defective; it was just that in her excitement she had "shot" off the whole film in a matter of seconds.

Sunlight brought a reflective gleam from the sea and brightness to the damp green summit of Boreray—to a sheep-cropped summit where the grass was now so fine it was as though an emerald green tablecloth had been spread over rock. The Kearton brothers mentioned the steep green slopes: slopes that ran upwards until they were lost "in the trailing skirts of a luminous white cloud."

Stac an Armin was like some vast twisted fang, its summit tickling the clouds at 644 feet. Stac Lee, at 564 feet, looked even more substantial. Each stack was speckled with the snow-white forms of gannets, each bird sitting just beyond beak-spiking range of its neighbours. Kittiwakes shouted their names as they swirled like snowflakes in a summer blizzard.

When the Kearton brothers were in these parts, they persuaded the St. Kildan fowlers to let them go on an outing to Boreray; they had landed from open boats on the water-smoothed rock and made a slow and difficult way to the main part of the island, clambering to an expanse of turf where puffins bred in vast numbers. "The clouds of birds that swept past us made a sound like a whirlwind whipping a great bed of dead rushes." So it is to-day. A hundred thousand puffins nest on Boreray.

Modern attempts to "storm the stacks" make use of Gemini (inflatable) craft. Every excursion is fraught with danger, and especially the first 100 feet of smooth rock on Stac an Armin, after which a visitor reaches a boulder slope, passing near (not through) the main gannet colony. Gannets, which are huge, share the stacks with several other species of bird, most surprisingly with the St. Kilda wren. The song of this tiny bird is a clarion call that is clearly heard above the general hub-bub.

Stac Lee was described by the Keartons as "one of the wonders of the world". In the year of their visit, this "Blue Stac" had been challenged by a young man called Heathcote; his sister climbed with him. The man wrote: "With the assistance of a rope and a sufficient amount of confidence, any active man could walk up the side of a house; but it needs a St. Kildan to get a foot-hold on an overhanging rock covered with slippery sea-weed and draw himself up to the top."

The seabirds nested uneasily when humans were about. St. Kilda was regularly visited by a steamer, the old *Dunara Castle*. The skipper arranged for the whistle to be blown to startle the seabirds into flight. The Keartons recorded an even more despicable trick: "As the boat came abreast of the towering rock, some members of the crew loaded and ran out a small brass cannon. The tip of a red-hot poker applied to the touch-hole of the gun produced a deafening explosion, which seemed to be instantly flung back at us by Stack Lee, and then thundered and reverberated from crag to crag along the rocky sides of Borrera, sending a great white cloud of startled gannets into the air above us."

How many eggs were broken or filched by predator birds during the

Mist-bonneted Boreray, four miles from the main island of Hirta.

time the startled birds were away from their nests will never be known. The loss must have been considerable.

We who sailed *MV Monaco* rejoiced at having a blink o'sun to enliven our colour photography and to show us what this archipelago looks like in good weather. As Cubby MacKinnon directed the *Monaco* towards Hirta, I looked back to see that the Weather Clerk had drawn a curtain of mist across the stacks. Within minutes they were blotted out. The visible world was reduced to a few hundred yards.

Our attention switched to Hirta and Dun. I was intrigued by the serrated ridge of Dun and by the fact that it was separated from Hirta by a channel that was little more than the width of a burn.

Hirta has huge, rounded hills that end abruptly with 1,000 ft cliffs. It is as though a giant has sliced them into two and removed half to make another island. On Hirta, an island for superlatives, Norse names are the language of topography—names that have a direct, no-nonsense meaning: Minastac for the Lesser Stack; Sgeir nan Sgarbh for Cormorant Rock, with a sprinkling of names including "geo", here and elsewhere, signifying a creek but in the St. Kildan setting more likely to be a tide-licked gully or even a sea-cave.

On our way to Village Bay, we saw rather than passed a pyramidical rock, Levenish, which had a great black backed gull as a feathered head-piece. The Keartons were to remember Levenish as the place where "the ship got the full benefit of wind and tide on her port, and, in consequence, rolled fearfully..." Yet no sooner had they got inside Village Bay than the sea "became almost as smooth as a mill-pond, and everybody was on deck, gazing intently at the weird scene."

This was the moment I had been dreaming about for half a century. The *Monaco* rounded, the Point of Coll. To the south, the long jagged ridge that is Dun was acting as a breakwater to the Atlantic swell. To the north lay Oiseval, the upper slopes covered with grey pimples which I later discovered were innumerable small stone storage chambers.

Ron Hardie organised the assembly of food and kit on a section of the deck that would be handy when the time came to load it on to the inflatable boats that would provide us with transport to the shore. I helped in fits and starts, anxious not to miss the approach to Village Bay.

Robert Atkinson, in my favourite Scottish book, *Island Going,* published in 1949, reports how he and his friends were held up by bad weather. Consequently they arrived in Village Bay at midnight. "As the ship came nearer and the night darkened, a rocky ridge stood out against a soft bowl of land behind. The ridge was Dun, guarding the south side of the bay. *Dunara Castle* drove wide round its point and, listing on the turn, steamed into Village Bay. Her siren blared and echoed round the enclosing dark hills. An answering light soon flickered from the amorphous hillside...

Village Bay, looking towards Dun, with part of the Army base in the foreground.

Men and dogs, photographed on Hirta in 1929.

"*Dunara's* anchor rattled down, steam hissed from the winch, a touch astern then, tinkle, tinkle, tinkle went the telegraph: Finished with Engines. A trip which should have taken seven or eight hours had come roundabout in nearly forty-eight, but the ship lay heaving gently in Village Bay."

After scanning the smooth rounded hills, with their coarse grasses, fan-like screes and stubble of heather, my eyes went directly to the concrete jetty, an improved version of the one where the St. Kildans huddled with their few possessions at Evacuation time, 60 years ago.

The Keartons described "a straggling line of primitive-looking dwellings". I winced at the sight of the Army base by the shore. The base was larger than I had imagined. In view was a generator house; the sound of the generator could be clearly heard across the water. A bungalow-like building was the officers' mess, and most of the other buildings appeared to be box-like. They had once been painted white and were now grey.

My eyes ranged hither and thither, looking for buildings that had become familiar to me through photographs—the Feather Store (yes, there it was, beside a shoreline of low cliffs), the minister's house (white-painted and now used as the sergeants' mess), and the factor's house (also white).

Much more satisfying was a view of the Street, a shallow crescent of cottages, the first five of which were roofed and looked well-cared-for. It had been enough, for the moment, to conserve the masonry of the other cottages to await their complete restoration. Visible between the cottages were the gable ends of the earlier dwellings which, sensibly, had been built side-on to the Bay—and the rain-bearing westerlies. Beyond the Street, within a grassy area enclosed by the substantial village wall, were innumerable cleits, those fascinating storage chambers. Most of them were in good order; they wore caps of living turf.

Along the shore, beyond a beach of summer sand, a wind-sock indicated a helicopter landing place. A modern road, gleaming white against the dun colours of the hillside, climbed in spectacular zig zags to where the skyline was cluttered with radomes and aerials.

Like the Psalmist of old, I gratefully lifted up mine eyes to the hills. In view was Conachair, a name signifying a meeting point of the hills. Conachair, at 1,396 ft., is the "attic" of Hirta, its seaward termination being the highest sea-cliff in Britain. Early settlers from Scandinavia named Oiseval (East Fell) and Ruaival (The Red Fell).

So much did I see and ponder about as our work party was landed and the previous work party embarked for the return to Oban. Cubby MacKinnon did not dawdle. Minutes later, with nae fuss, nae bother—just a cheery wave—he directed his boat towards the open sea.

During the next fortnight, I must have scanned the bay a thousand times and not once was it devoid of craft. The visiting boats would include an Army landing craft with supplies, naval auxiliaries, a vessel being used by the Nature Conservancy Council, the *Jean de la Lune,* a Dutch trawler with an injured man who needed attention ashore, a cabin cruiser from Ulster, various sailing boats—and a canoe that had been paddled across 36 miles of open sea (more later).

Part of the Street on Hirta in 1929, shortly before the Evacuation.

A Walk Along the Street

WORK PARTY NO. 3 was transported to shore by inflatable craft, along with a variety of goods and possessions. Some of us shared a boat with a box holding cabbages, leeks and bananas, and one of those ubiquitous plastic bread containers—this one actually holding bread.

It was a moment of high excitement to actually set foot on Hirta, even though the patch of concrete on to which I stepped had probably been laid in recent times as part of the considerable modification to the pier.

I shouldered some bags and followed others beside the generator building, around which hung a faint blue haze. I passed an incinerator, with its blackened brickwork, and the toilet-and-shower block to be used by both sexes.

Twenty minutes had passed and I did not feel to be on the island of my dreams. Then the Old St. Kilda asserted itself. The Factor's House was visited—so that we might store food in a capacious refrigerator. The way now led along a pleasant path near a wall which ancient hands had formed of stones made without a dab of mortar.

Oystercatchers, the pied pipers of St. Kilda, noisily protested at my intrusion and fluttered around while their downy young "froze" to escape detection.

I carried my kit-bag to the "bothy" that had been allocated to the men of the party. My feet encountered what was to me the sacred turf of the Street, a thoroughfare, open to the meadows and the Bay on one side and, on the other, flanked by what remains of blackhouses, cleits, crofts and ruined Victorian cottages.

The "bothy" was a restored cottage, devoid now of partitioning walls and having a fireplace at either end. The walls were grey, the windows small, the door somewhat stiff—which is a "good fault" in an area noted for its blustering winds.

Robert Atkinson took these photographs of three St. Kildans on their return to Hirta for part of the summer of 1938. They are Mrs. Gillies and Neil Gillies *(above)*, Finlay MacQueen and Neil Gillies (below).

I dropped the kit-bag on a metal-framed bed and resumed my walk along the Street. It meandered amiably. I could not take it all in at a single glance.

Sixteen cottages were to be seen—most of them open to the sky, but in a curious way having dignity even in decay. These cottages were built in the 1860s, following damage to property caused by a storm that was severe even in St. Kildan terms.

John Ross, a master-mason brought from the mainland, supervised the work. The style was to be unashamedly Scottish—two ee's (eyes = windows) and a moo' (mouth = door). The wood was imported. On St. Kilda, anything that grows higher than a dock leaf is called a tree!

Robert Atkinson, on his visit to St. Kilda in July, 1938, had the great privilege of meeting some of the former inhabitants, who had returned for a summer stay. He met Neil Gillies, a middle-aged man with a gammy leg, and his mother, Mrs John Gillies. He encountered that great celebrity, Finlay MacQueen.

Robert Atkinson photographed Mrs Gillies as she operated a spinning wheel outside No. 11. Neil was portrayed at the Post Office, a second picture showing him sitting before the fire in the old family cottage—sitting on a simple wooden chair, two legs of which rested on a mat, before a smouldering fire that held a number of pans and had a cluttered mantelpiece, above which hung a framed print of some stylish Edwardian beauty.

Hirta is rich in the remains of ancient peoples. The oldest structure in the area of the village appears to be The Earth-house (though it might have been an ice-house). It fascinated Richard Kearton, who noted: "The dwelling is something in the form of a huge drain . . . the entrance to which commands an excellent view of Village Bay. This last fact was, no doubt, of great importance, in order that the people might have early knowledge of the approach of enemies."

This "house", in the form of a subterranean tunnel, was walled on each side, with flags on the floor and a drain below the flags. It was known to the St. Kildans as House of the Fairies.

Calum Mor's house, of about 600 AD, is partly underground. The visible part, made of huge stones, is domed, the dome being overspread with turf to keep out the wind. Stones placed on the turf gave the structure the appearance of a currant pudding.

When Martin Martin voyaged to St. Kilda in 1697, the common type of house was thatched. Two rows of such houses faced one another across the High Street, which was a causeway of stone. About a century later, the primitive appearance of the Village was commented on by Lord Brougham. He landed on Hirta at Glen Bay. His party explored the Glen and then

41

climbed the shoulder of Am Blaid.

From here they had a breath-taking view of Oiseval, Village Bay—and the Village itself. "In the centre of a small bay surrounded by an immense amphitheatre of mountains lies the village of St. Kilda which from the height where we stood looked like a cluster of bee-hives, nor should we have recognised them as houses but for the smoke which arose from them in thick columns."

What I had thought of as "blackhouses" were the improved buildings that took shape in the 1830s. People and stock lived under a single capacious roof, for each incorporated a byre, a living area and sleeping quarters.

The thatched roof fascinated a visitor in 1841; he wrote: "They have circular or somewhat rounded roofs of thatch, well fastened down with ropes of the same material, and instead of the straw overhanging the walls, as is usual in the low countries, and affording an effectual purchase for the wind to lay hold of, the edge of the thatch springs from the inner side of the thick wall, and so the wind blowing up its outside, and there finding

Visitors to the Street. A picture from "The Oban Times" of 1930.

42

A modern working party of the National Trust for Scotland gathers at a restored building to be given their tasks for the day.

nothing else to act upon, instead of carrying off the roof as it would otherwise be apt to do, simply slips over this cupola kind of covering..."

My walk along the Street began outside the Factor's House, where I chatted about puffins with Jim, the NCC warden. In the early stages of the walk, I was sworn at by the ubiquitous oystercatcher and I panicked one of the Soay sheep, a particularly flighty breed. The sheep made off at high speed, leaving a tuft of last winter's coat, for it was moulting time.

Five cottages had been restored by the National Trust for Scotland and were used by visiting work-parties. Cottage No. 1 had become a kitchen, dining room, common room and party leader's quarters, these amenities being spread across one large room and a very small one. Cottage No. 1 was the nightly playground of St. Kilda mice, which—when Cook was not around—were enticed by heaps of bread or biscuits.

Cottage No. 2 was the women's dormitory, a smaller room being used by Cook and yet more St. Kilda mice which entered and left the room through a sizeable gap under the door.

Cottage No. 3 was now converted into a museum of local life, which I visited daily to sketch some of the fascinating objects. The museum, with its modernistic layout, astonished visitors to this "wild and remote" island. Here, one evening, I was joined by a lad from Devon who had just

43

joined the Army contingent on Hirta. Some Irish visitors who asked for directions to the museum entered it with considerable delight. Another time, it was being occupied by half a dozen military gentlemen—some visiting generals, soon to be taken off the island by helicopter.

Cottage No. 4, the men's dormitory, was the building with a gale-warped door that opened protestingly. The grating sound might be heard at intervals of one or two hours by day or night as people kept to their own routines and took advantage of this far-northern island where in summer the night has shrunk to a few darkish hours.

To leave the old cottage for a trip to the toilet block was not irksome: I would stroll along the Street, with the moon hanging like a lantern over Village Bay and the night air shivering with the "bleating" of snipe. There is a touch of magic in the Hebridean night.

Cottage No. 5, a workroom with space for archaeological material, also served as a shipyard: more precisely, a place for making St. Kilda Mailboats so that postcards of St. Kilda could start their journey to friends and relatives in a traditional way, bobbing on the waves as they were tide and wind-borne to the Hebrides.

A fulmar petrel patrolled the Street, passing me silently, at a range of half a dozen yards. St. Kilda wrens poured out their hearts in songs. Every blackhouse and cleit appeared to have its nesting pair of starlings and I marvelled at the ability of one adult bird to shout abuse at me when it had a beak stuffed with food. The churring of young birds was so common as to provide a constant background noise.

An alert oystercatcher. The strident voice of this pied bird with the red bill punctuates the Hirtan day in spring and summer.

Patriarchs in the Village, photographed by Frank Lowe in 1929.

Meanwhile, oystercatchers with young greeted each Army jogger with their strident alarm calls as the keep-fit enthusiasts followed courses a little higher up the slope.

I entered Cottage No. 13, where Frank and Betty Lowe of Bolton told me they had stayed in 1929. They lodged with a widow; they shared their bedroom with St. Kilda mice, which had been known to nest in the bed! The Lowes bartered a tin of solidified methylated spirits for some insect powder in the hope of driving the mice to other quarters.

The cottage was recalled as being small, low and crudely finished, with one door. The floors were rotten with damp and the walls papered with nothing better than sheets of newspaper. (I was to learn that this was not the general custom). The main room was heated by a fire in an open grate, a cauldron hanging over the glowing peat. Nearby was a spinning wheel, also a gannet wing being used as a sweeping brush.

Their landlady made bread from flour and carbonate of soda, slowly cooking it in large slabs, portions of which were torn off as required. Yeast was unknown here. The cottage was illuminated by a crude lamp—a gannet's stomach, filled with fulmar oil, with a gannet's quill acting as the wick.

Richard and Cherry Kearton, visiting Hirta rather more than 90 years ago, opted for the Factor's house. After sweeping out plaster that had fallen off the walls during the preceding 12 months, and lighting a fire in the grateless hearth, they began to set things to rights. "The place being half buried in the base of a steep hill called Oiseval was fearfully damp, and when my brother, with the instinct of a photographer, commenced to prowl round in search of a 'dark' room, the boards were in such a rotten condition on the ground floor that he fell through.''

The Keartons recalled the Street itself in relation to the strong smell of fulmar oil, the plenitude of birds' wings and feathers on the midden heaps, and the numbers of birds' eggs that adorned almost every window sill. They mentioned the curious all-wood locks on the cowhouse doors (a type of lock collected by Frank and Betty Lowe and now in my possession). Richard Kearton bought one as a curiosity and he attempted to describe its workings.

Alice Shawcross, the daughter of a Fleetwood trawlerman, mentioned the time she stayed overnight in a St. Kildan cottage during the 1920s. Her father, Skipper Carter, was giving two of his children and another boy a holiday treat—a fishing expedition to St Kilda. Dropping anchor in Village Bay, he took the youngsters ashore, where he himself delivered mail to the Post Office.

Alice recalled that as the small boat came alongside the jetty, one or two people stood at their doors and watched the Fleetwood party clamber ashore. The island air was fragrant with the reek of peat, which was being burnt as fuel in the cottages. She saw the fine figure of Finlay MacQueen, complete with long white beard. The crew on the trawler had a nickname for anyone who wore such a long beard—Nitty Whiskers.

The weather having worsened, it was decided that the children would stay ashore overnight. Alice thus experienced the typical St. Kildan hospitality, provided in this case by a branch of the large Gillies family. Dad told the youngsters not to venture from the vicinity of the house, in case the trawler had to leave in a hurry; ''He did not want us to be a nuisance to anyone.''

Alice was impressed by the stillness of the Street as compared with a typical street in Fleetwood, where children played noisily. ''On St. Kilda no children stirred.'' She and the two lads washed their necks and cleaned their teeth. They were then allocated a bedroom with ''proper'' paper on the walls. Alice recalls that it had tiny pink rosebuds on it. ''We had been told that people on the island used newspapers to cover the walls.'' The bed allocated to the children was large, with an iron frame and brass knobs. The mattress was stuffed with feathers. The bedding was spotless.

They slept in their clothes. ''I didn't take anything off except my boots and sou'wester. I got into bed wearing my coat and I remember thinking that if we had to run for the boat, I would at least be half-dressed.'' It was a noisy bed. ''Every time anyone moved, that bed more than squeaked; it groaned and shrieked. It talked to us!''

Above: Frank Lowe, who visited St. Kilda with his wife Betty in 1929, and Alice Shawcross (nee Carter) who was here on an outing by trawler from Fleetwood a few years earlier. *Below:* Frank Lowe's study of a cottage interior on Hirta.

Next morning the hospitable Gillies family provided Scotch pancakes. These proved to be too rich for the Lancashire children and caused stomach upsets. "They made me poorly—and I'd done so well. We were given cups of tea. The water came from a spring and was nice and pure . . . We had a basin to wash in and each of us was given a clean towel to wipe our hands and face. Mind you, we only had a quick swill."

At daybreak, they heard the steam whistle of the trawler. The children were on the jetty as the ship's boat came across the shining bay.

Back at Fleetwood, Alice wrote an essay at school on her St. Kildan experiences. "I got 9 out of 10 for it . . . I don't think that St. Kilda will ever be forgotten among the fishing fraternity."

After the Evacuation, the Fleetwood trawlers sheltered in Village Bay and sometimes men went ashore. In 1947, Jack Kelly—who was in these waters as skipper of the *Wyre Corsair*—found the Street was "a lonesome sight". He entered the Church and saw that the Bible on the pulpit was in good condition, which surprised him; the place was full of mice.

In earlier times, Jack Kelly had marvelled at the stamina of the local people. "St. Kilda was always important to Fleetwood fishermen, but when you saw how the people lived, it made you wonder how they managed to bring up their families and survive there for so long . . ."

Mrs Cora Jinks was to recall for the *Evening Gazette* that in 1912 she spent three days at St. Kilda. She loved the sea and had her first voyage on a trawler when she was only five years old. Spending some time ashore, she noticed that the islanders baked potatoes in the turf fires and made flat cakes of soda bread. They were friendly and hospitable. She had but one regret. When her trawlerman father came back to collect the young people, Cora was nursing a pet lamb. She wept when told she would not be able to take it back to Fleetwood.

So to the present time. We mustered at No. 1 the Street for our meals, the first a lunchtime snack of tuna, corned beef, oatcake bread and salad, with cheese and biscuits to follow; there was also fruit. Several trestle tables, pushed together, provided a surface large enough to accommodate all 12 of us and the leader.

In the old days, this cottage had been occupied by the McKinnons, who took possession of the place when it was built in 1859. The first resident was Lachlan McKinnon; either this man or another Lachlan was here in 1883. At the time of the Evacuation, Norman McKinnon sorrowfully closed the door for what he must have believed to have been the last time. Now, by courtesy of the National Trust for Scotland, there was still a door, also windows holding glass, and a roof which our efforts would reinforce against the rigours of the coming St. Kildan winter.

The building was full of chatter as we mustered for our meals—a mixed

A member of a National Trust for Scotland working party busy roofing a cottage.

bunch: doctor, dentist, midwife, retired vet, archivist, industrial designer, researcher, men connected with the building industry and myself, a retired Editor, qualified for nothing but willing to do anything. In the event, I could lend a hand with many a job.

The real do-it-yourself types spent some hot, calm days on the roof of No. 1, slowly unrolling felt coated with bitumen and stroking the bitumen with a blow-lamp for adhesion. Their chants and the roar of the blowlamp punctuated the otherwise languid days. Eventually, the nail-tappers joined them and produced a sound like demented woodpeckers at their nesting trees in spring.

It pleased me to know that the traditional type of Hebridean Cottage roof was favoured. Originally, it was of zinc, but ''it rained inside whenever it rained outside'' so this was replaced by felt painted with pitch and held down with metal straps on battens which passed over the roof and were attached to spikes driven into the walls.

Each day, two people were delegated to help Linda, the Cook. These workers soon heard about the St. Kilda Go-fer, which is not the second cousin of the celebrated St. Kilda mouse, but a person given kitchen duties; he or she would be expected, when requested, to ''go-fer this and go-fer that...''

The nightly gavortings of mice continued to engage our interest. Ron said: "It's important to snore to keep the mice away." The St. Kilda house mouse became extinct, its place being taken by the special island form of the long-tailed field mouse, descended, it is believed, from animals that came with the Vikings. (The St. Kilda mouse thus has relatives in Norway and Iceland).

Mice were especially common in the Street; they visited the dining room area nightly, from about 10pm and were reported to be scuttering outdoors by revellers returning from the *Puff-Inn* at the Army complex to their civilian quarters by moonlight. These revellers assured us that their sightings were not induced by strong drink. And that the mice they saw were greyish, not pink!

St. Kilda field mouse, which occupies the niche left when the local variety of the house mouse became extinct.

Ron took us on a tour of the village area. It began, surprisingly, with a rusting gun, which was installed towards the end of the 1914-18 war after a German submarine appeared in Village Bay and lobbed a few shells in anger. One of the shells struck the Feather Store and dramatically shortened it; another demolished the Post Office, which would not have been difficult; it was made largely of zinc. The gun on St. Kilda was never fired in anger and has now rusted up.

And here was the kirk, splendidly restored, maintained immaculately, with an adjacent schoolroom that looked as though it had just been tidied up after the day's work. Writing-slates had been put away neatly. The Victorian interest in North America, largely from the point of view of emigration, was indicated by the map on the wall—a map of Canada.

The Burial Ground on Hirta as it was about 1930.

Ron's tour included Cottage No. 16, with a simple incised cross, which came to light in recent times following a fall of plaster. Who first brought Christianity to St. Kilda? Could it have been one or more of the gentle but determined Celtic monks, en route from Ireland to Iceland?

We entered the graveyard, where the tiny Christ's Church had stood. It was built entirely of stone and its dimensions were a mere 24 feet by 14 feet. The present kirk was its successor, round about 1830, at which time a connecting Manse was built. A visitor in 1884 was to recall its barn-like appearance, the rough forms and the floor of "cold, damp, black earth". Carpenters working on the new school in 1898 fitted a wooden floor to the church.

The present kirk has what is reputed to be the largest pulpit in the Western Isles. Still vividly recalled through stories of the old days are the 24 years of the Rev John MacKay, under whose influence the formal practice of religion dominated almost entirely the St. Kildan way of life, to the extent that the islanders had scarcely enough free time to follow such old occupations as fishing and fowling whereby they had been self-reliant.

John Sands, concerned at the minister's egotistical manner and over-strict rule, wrote: "The weak-minded pope and prime minister rolled into one who rules the destinies of the island has reduced religion into a mere hypocritical formalism, finding no place in his creed for self-reliance or any of the manlier virtues. . . It is nothing to Mr MacKay whether the poor people starve in their crofts or neglect the fishing so long as his own silly fads are observed."

The islanders appear to have found in the religious life, however stern, a happy release from the daily round and common task.

Cleits on Hirta. The total number is in excess of 1,200. *Above:* St. Kildans attend to the masonry of a damaged cleit in 1929. *Below:* A fine study by Robert Atkinson, one of a collection taken in the summer of 1938.

A Soay ram.

Sods, Cleits and Sheep Dung

EACH WORKDAY, we gathered outside Cottage No. 1. Ron allocated jobs informally and with good humour. We were not being subjected to forced labour. It was in the spirit of the old St. Kildan "Parliament", which had met each morning except on the Sabbath to discuss mutual affairs and to plan the day's activities.

Gladstone, a visitor in 1927, mentioned such matters as the weeding of potatoes or the rounding up of sheep; the despatch of a boat to Boreray for sheep-shearing or the collection of crotol [used in the dyeing of wool]. It was this grave-looking assembly of men who, in 1930, discussed the most important topic any of them had had to face—the possibility of Evacuation to the mainland. Three years earlier, the Parliament had been functioning as usual. "Often the talking went on until well after mid-day, but when the decision was made everyone settled down to the job in hand until it was finished."

And so did we. Ron mentioned the re-roofing of Cottage No. 1. He discussed with a former joiner the production of shutters for the Feather Store and the flooring of part of Cottage No. 5. Emissaries, with mops, buckets and bleach, were sent to the toilet block. And I was among those detailed to work on the tops of cleits that had been eroded by the wind and needed some replenishment of turf.

My first working period was thus devoted to "sods, cleits and sheep dung". As one group of cheerful labourers began to lay more bitumised felt on the roof of Cottage No. 1, and as another applied himself to carpentry, I collected a spade and a wheelbarrow marked: NTS, ST. KILDA and trundled it to the first cleit on the list.

The way led over a sward that had the June sunshine upon it; I could almost hear that grass growing. So numerous and varied were the cleits that on two occasions I lost sight of the rest of the party.

We began work at the third cleit. Our first had been tenanted by oystercatchers; the nest with its eggs occupied an unusual site on top of a crumbling wall. To disturb the birds would have been unthinkable. They cried so stridently, I felt they were more likely to have disturbed *us!*

At the second cleit, we had come under the unblinking gaze of a fulmar. The name of this common petrel comes from the Norse *Fyl-mare,* signifying a creature that spits. As the fulmar began the gulping process that would lead to its parting with a jet of amber-coloured oil, we picked up our spades and barrows and retreated.

The third cleit was devoid of fulmar, wren and starling. Hirta has a bountiful bird life. As we walked across broken ground towards the cleit, we annoyed another pair of oystercatchers and flushed several snipe, which gave the sneezy sound of alarm as they zig-zagged in the air.

The area of the major cleits, between the Street and boundary wall of the Village, was carpeted with several inches of soil held together by grass in a vigorous stage of growth—a sod-seeker's paradise. We had to show care in our choice of site, however, and eventually lifted turf from the bed of a minor watercourse.

Soay sheep looked up mournfully as we advanced. The sleek new coat was in view here and there. Where it was not visible, the old hair clung in tufts. These primitive sheep had just suffered a dramatic numerical decline. Over the winter and into spring, some 50% of the animals had died from starvation and illness. This was Nature's way of ensuring the survival of the fittest. The population on Hirta had risen to well over 1,700 which was more than the land could sustain in an average winter.

The survivors and their bonnie lambs, some chestnut, some black, cropped the lush summer grass. The rams and ewes moulted their winter coat as they ate. On St. Kilda, the Soay sheep are permitted to live naturally, with a minimum of interference from humans.

Enterprising sheep took advantage of the Army presence by visiting the place near the generating plant where pipes were set a few feet from the ground—at a height suited to back-scratching! It was not unusual to see half a dozen sheep thus engaged and to watch the old wool come away in large tufts.

Family groups of sheep dined in the old Village meadows, across the hills and also on cliffs, frequenting places where I would have expected

The common snipe is, indeed, common about the Village.

them to suffer from vertigo. The lambs do their best to keep up with the ewes; the ravens and hooded crows take any sickly or weak stock.

I watched a large chestnut lamb and a slightly smaller black lamb meeting each other spiritedly, and doubtless a little painfully, head to head. One lamb gave way, turned and began to graze submissively. The other promptly butted it on the rump. David, a vet., said: "That chestnut lamb should prosper!"

In the old days, cleits were protected against sheep by having doors; nowadays, almost all the cleits are available as shelter. Thick layers of compacted droppings indicate the duration and scale of the occupation. Sheep seek out cleits as dormitories on stormy nights. Others drop their lambs in cleits. And the aged or infirm sheep may crawl into the nearest cleits to die. Their memorials are tufts of wool and heaps of bleached skeletons.

A young woman who was conducting detailed research into Soay sheep was to be seen at all hours as she trailed groups of animals and watched them through binoculars. When she saw a sheep defacate, she noted the number on the animal's ear tag and collected the droppings for later analysis.

At night, this student of the Soay, quietly cornered sheep in some of the cleits and placed bright tags on their ears for ready identification. Ear-clipping was an old Norse custom and is still used by northern flockmasters; this "law" mark became a "lug" mark, and lug in northern England is just another name for ear. Years ago, a naughty child in Yorkshire had his or her "lugs clattered"! The tags used on Hirta would be easier to see than traditional marks.

One night, our sheep-watcher appeared at the door of a bothy with a ram. One of its eyes was threatened by an unusually well-curved horn; the tip of the horn was promptly sawn off and the old ram went gruntingly back into the darkness.

But mainly, the sheep were left to their own devices. I hope the student did not see one of the soldiers at the cookhouse surreptitiously feeding his favourite animal, which came to him when called! Or overhear someone say that Soay mutton is so strong it tastes like venison. Needless to say, it had not been tasted on St. Kilda, where all forms of life are conserved.

Cleit with its guardian fulmar near the Feather Store on Hirta.

On sunny evenings, I often walked among the cleits behind The Street and marvelled at how anything so attractive could have evolved in the isolation of these Atlantic islands, for if they are found elsewhere, I cannot put a name to it.

Here were structures eminently fitted for their purpose, made of the handiest available stone—white granite or the darker breccia—and sharing the general characteristics of being low-set, oblong in form, with high crowns topped by living turf watered by the frequent Hebridean showers and never likely to degenerate into dust.

The turf roof, resting on stone slabs, absorbed the rain. The drystone walls kept out the rain but permitted the wind to pass through, keeping the contents of the cleit dry.

Our job was to cut sods and transport them to a cleit which had a less than complete covering of turf. Meanwhile, sheep dung taken from the handiest cleit was used to fertilise the bared ground: another crop of grass soon appeared.

To sit in the cool and shady recess of a cleit when there was no one else about was to be able to appreciate something of the life-style of early Christian hermits—they who left their native Ireland for rock stacks, islets and larger but under-populated lands. In the absence of a cave, a hermit would use whatever material was to hand for his cell; he would then joyfully devote most of his time to prayer and praise.

Perhaps the style of the hermit's lodgings was that from which the cleit of today developed; it was first used as a home and then, as better styles were developed, became a storage or drying chamber. Martin Martin, the intrepid 17th century visitor, wrote of "stone pyramidal houses" or "pyramids". He saw "some hundreds" on Hirta. (Over 1,200 have been surveyed by the archaeologist Mary Harman).

The pimply structures on Oiseval and Conachair served simply as storage; so, too, were those to be seen on the near-vertical boulder slope of Carn Mor, the nesting place of countless petrels and puffins, where some long-forgotten St. Kildan had simply set an inclined slab against a drystone wall. The structure is now used by naturalists on their all night vigils. The cleit sleeps two people—if they do not breathe too deeply!

The white granite of St. Kilda, like the limestone of my native Yorkshire, has the chameleon-like ability to change its hue according to the prevailing conditions. Such a cleit is bone-white in sunlight, golden as the summer sun begins to set and silvery in the light of the moon. When wet, in sunset, the stones have a purplish hue.

I asked Mary Harman about the type of objects that were stored in cleits; she mentioned hay, corn, latterly potatoes, dried birds and the eggs of seabirds preserved in peat ash. Corn or grass were simply tossed loosely undercover as soon as it was cut. It would dry under cover. Richard Kearton wrote: "The wind rushes through the side-walls at a furious rate— as I can testify, having spent a night in one—and dries whatever is placed in them."

Into the cleits, outside the fowling season, would go the vital long ropes used for fowling. A rope stored in damp conditions would soon become mouldy and useless. Some cleits near the village might be used for the storage of manure. Others had clothes hanging in them. In the newer cottages built in the Street—those houses which had their windows and doors facing the prevailing wind and rain—condensation was a recurring problem. (It did not happen in the old blackhouses, where the principal hazard would be from firesmoke).

While examining some cleits on the hill, I located a few turves of peat, cut over 60 years before, confirming yet another use to which these strange but practical little structures, had been put. Every St. Kildan used a number of cleits in proportion to the area of land rented from the steward. Every cleit near the village has now been recorded and numbered. I became a member of the exclusive 123 Club when I crawled from the cleit bearing that number to its bee hive-shaped annexe.

We were expected to work four hours a day; in fact, the routine was varied to suit the weather. On some days, we worked through the day; on the following day we relaxed or explored Hirta. There are no unsociable hours during the St. Kildan summer. In the wee small hours, I was listening for storm petrels when the local oystercatchers created a racket of strident sounds. I looked towards the hill. The form of a runner was sillhouetted at its rim.

Those who worked by day and stayed on their feet for most of the night appeared at breakfast with puffy eyes and ashy complexion. One late reveller, lying in his bed five minutes before breakfast-time, remarked huskily: "I'm just going through in my mind's eye what I'll do when the bell goes..."

The lives of the St. Kildans were divided into bed, work and kirk, with little time for pleasure as such. In the deepest part of the winter, the women were engaged in spinning and weaving; the men spent the short days at various tasks, including the shifting of peat turves to places handy to the house.

Food was especially scarce in late winter and the early spring, when the three simple meals a day consisted of such staples as porridge, dried fulmar flesh (sometimes boiled in porridge—ugh!) and cheese.

The diet improved with the arrival of spring. Now the cattle could be turned on to the inland—which would make the air somewhat sweeter in the old blackhouses where people and stock lived under the same roof.

Life on Hirta in 1929. Frank Lowe took these photographs of outdoor spinning and three barefooted children.

Birds which had been widely spread across the northern seas used their astonishing navigational aids to re-locate St. Kilda and to arrive in their thousands to nest. It was possible by March to catch a few guillemots for food.

By April, the cattle were in the outfield, gannets and puffins had been added to the household menu and some thought was given to preparing the land for cultivation. Meanwhile, in April (and on until August) turf was being cut to provide winter fuel on treeless Hirta.

Seabirds were by now to be counted in millions. Every suitable ledge on the 1,000 ft cliffs of Hirta was colonised by fulmars. The distant stacks were whitened by the forms of gannets and the birds' excrement. In May, using the big boat, men went after fulmars, gannets and the eggs of puffins; in June and July, puffins were the main prey, followed in August and September by young fulmars, and in September and October by the young gannets.

As the birds dispersed across the ocean, the St. Kildans used their reserve supplies of food, including the dried corpses of birds which they had stored in the cleits. Cattle were brought in for the winter. Once again, the clack and whir of the spinning wheel and the loom were to be heard as winter arrived with its usual darkness and climatic ferocity and good tweed was produced for barter or sale the following summer.

A gannet with young. The species was once known as Solan-Goose.

The sign of the Puff-inn, within the military establishment on Hirta. Its "good cheer" is dispensed to soldier and visitor alike. It has low prices and flexible opening hours!

Today, an attack of melancholia induced by the persistent howl of the wind or a "wee shower" lasting for days can be offset by a visit to St. Kilda's pub, the most westerly in Britain. It is called the *Puff-inn* and features the celebrated bird. According to a National Trust for Scotland leaflet, the *Puff-inn* is "famous (or infamous) for its low prices and flexible opening hours..."

On my first visit I opened the door onto bright lights and heard a tumult of chattering and the clink of many glasses. Next time, only one voice at a time might be heard. The lads were watching an American film that was being projected on a wall. The curtains had been drawn as a formality; nothing could entirely blot out the power of the summer sunshine, even at such a late hour as this.

I order a Coke in a whisper, so as not to compete with the drawling voices on the Hollywood soundtrack. Silently, I find a spare seat as the patrons of the *Puff-inn* concentrate on the huge images produced by the noisy projector.

Bored after three minutes, I let my eyes wander along other walls, which were decked by photographs, amusing notices and a shredded Union Jack which, I heard, had been brand-new when raised on the mast, only to be stuck there for days as a gale roared about Hirta. When eventually the flag could be recovered, it was ruined beyond repair.

The film ended. Normal chatter was resumed. I heard some of the modern tales of St. Kilda, such as the airdrop of supplies from a Cessna aircraft and of how one container came apart. A bystander was struck and seriously injured—by a frozen chicken!

The Cessna was operating from the airfield on the western (the flattest) part of Benbecula, a small island sandwiched between North Uist on one side and South Uist on the other. A friend who served on Benbecula in the late 1970s, told me that the atmosphere was sometimes so clear, he might see St. Kilda from the visual room at the top of the control tower. "Inevitably, there was a local saying that if you could see St. Kilda it was going to rain and if you couldn't see St. Kilda, it was raining."

He summed up the weather as "wet and windy", adding: "The most noticeable feature is the strength of the wind. It's an area where the rain can come horizontally. When I arrived, I was told of a controller who, during a gale, had to get out of his car and crawl to the control tower on all fours... It was a rare sight when the windsock was motionless."

Each month, there were two regular trips to the Army base on St. Kilda. One was the mail drop. A twin-engined aircraft was chartered to take a sack of mail. It was an ordinary Post Office sack in a heavy leather-bag. Over Hirta, a trap in the floor of the fuselage was opened up and an Army sergeant had to judge the appropriate time to drop the sack so that it hit the top of the hill and could be recovered by waiting soldiers.

"The very first time I went down to St. Kilda, I discovered that the pilot was a new man who had not done this mail trip before. I was trying to map-read for him. There was a new Army sergeant, so we were all green. We did the run-in and the Army lads stood on top of the cliff to receive the mail.

"The pilot was a bit scared he was going to hit them with this sack, which would have been lethal from the height we were flying. He must have given the order at slightly the wrong moment and the Army sergeant dropped the sack—straight over the cliff edge. We did several circuits after that and eventually located the sack; it had dropped on a ledge. The men on the island had to get the ropes out and lower someone over the cliffs to retrieve the mail."

I asked him for his impressions of St. Kilda from the air. He replied: "I was amazed that a community had existed there. Looking at it from the air, it is like a stone in the middle of the ocean."

My reverie at the *Puff-inn* about air transport to St. Kilda ended when a soldier mentioned another potentially amusing occupation—Drunken Draughts, played on the floor, with half pints of lager to represent the

An eider duck on its nest, which is lagged with down plucked from its breast. On the nest, this brownish bird looks like a feathered tea cosy.

pieces. Any piece captured was promptly drunk!

For some soldiers, the *Puff-inn* offered warmth, colour and comradeship. It was here that plans were made for bizarre competitions, such as that for catching sheep, the principal requirement for a competitor being the ability to "run like hell!"

After a spell dawdling over a single Coke, I wandered down to the beach and listened to the cooing of the eiders—ah-oo-ah. Across the bay, gannets were circling and diving. Two cheerful soldiers were fishing on the "chuck it in and chance it" principle. It had worked for them; they had caught a codling.

I was overcome by sadness at the knowledge that this jetty was the gathering point for St. Kildans when, in 1930, they were evacuated to new homes on the mainland.

There was a happy moment during my stay on St. Kilda when a canoeist of more than average ability and bravery arrived. That evening,

David Hayter, who paddled a canoe for 36 miles from Haskeir in the Western Isles to Village Bay, Hirta, is pictured here with the canoe he used. Much valuable equipment, including his navigator, had been damaged when he landed on Haskeir in turbulent conditions.

a barbecue was being held outside the officers' mess. The lads in the *Puff-inn* were on their third rounds of drinks when David Hayter appeared in Village Bay. He had just paddled 36 miles from the Hebrides.

David left Lochmaddy, North Uist, on June 1. The wind, though light at Force Four, was coming from the north. David was slowed down as he fought his way round into the Sound of Harris. He reached an uninhabited island as a storm arrived and for two nights was confined to his tent. Then near-perfect conditions arrived. A strong easterly wind speeded him for the island of Haskeir, from which he would make the last 36 mile voyage to St. Kilda.

He neared Haskeir in turbulent conditions. He had a difficult task landing on a cliffbound coastline. Using climbing equipment, he was inching the canoe up a steep rock shelf when the rope parted. Both David and the canoe fell 25 feet into the sea; the canoe was caught in the undertow and swept under an overhang. Much of its vital equipment, including the nagivator, was damaged.

David inflated his lifejacket and kept afloat. He was hurt, having pulled the ligaments in his right shoulder, which meant it had little movement. He was exhausted after his efforts. None the less, he got his canoe clear of the water.

When he took stock, he realised he had lost half of his supply of fresh water. It was greatly depleted during the four days he was stormbound on Haskeir. His radio still operated. The skipper of a local fishing boat, *Achieve,* despite the stormy conditions, supplied him with four litres of water.

By June 7, radio weather forecasts indicated the approach of a "window" in the weather. He would risk the final 36 mile crossing to St. Kilda. David used ropes to manoeuvre his canoe into the water. At 12.45 pm, Haskeir was left behind. He headed into the Atlantic, where good weather conditions obtained.

He faced a 20 foot swell but the sea did not run across it and although the wind was variable, it never rose above Force Three. His radio was dead, so he could not signal his approach to Hirta. He was, however, spotted when far out at sea. There was time for a small crowd to gather and extend their congratulations as he drew alongside the pier at 10 pm.

David lingered on the pier to watch "one of the most glorious sunsets I have ever seen", before joining the barbecue as the guest of Captain Ball, the Station Commander on St. Kilda.

I made my way slowly back to the bothy in the gloaming and experienced something of the old atmosphere of Hirta. Admittedly, one heard the thump of the generator at the military base, where night was day through the use of sodium chloride lighting. But, having my back to modernity, I could thrill to the grey serenity of the Street, where gliding fulmars were so proprietorial they might almost have been reincarnated villagers.

A snipe was "drumming", diving in the still air, extending the outer feathers of its tail and permitting the air to rush through the stiffened barbs with a bleating sound.

I heard the strident piping from oystercatchers disturbed by yet more late-night joggers.

An Army jogger, with weighted belt, traverses the Street on his way to the hill.

An Atlantic seal.

Looking for the Tunnel

RON ANNOUNCED that he was leading an expedition to The Tunnel. It was strange to hear an English placename on an island where Norse words predominate.

By taking us to The Tunnel, Ron also introduced us to Hirta's volcanic grandeur. What we now call St. Kilda are fragments of the rim of an ancient volcano that flared about 60 million years ago. This was violence on the grand scale. Other centres of volcanic activity were Rum, Ardnamurchan, Mull, Arran and Ulster.

No human observed the Big Bangs of ancient times but they were to have their echoes in folklore. Fingal occupied his (volcanic) cave on Staffa and a Giant bestrode his dolerite pavement just across the sea in Northern Ireland.

What nature gave, amid flame, smoke and dust, nature has since taken away. At St. Kilda, the familiar volcanic shape has gone, blasted into oblivion. The lava flows have cooled, cracked and vanished. Ash that rained down, to become compacted, was not tough enough to resist frost, wind and waves.

The St. Kilda of today will in due course be obliterated. On Hirta, the island will be broken down, with Mullach Bi, Conachair and Oiseval becoming separate entities. Each will then be sea-licked to the size of a stack. Each stack will topple. And of course, there will be no human to observe the last traces of St. Kilda.

The headland where the Tunnel lies is to the east of Glen Bay, on the north coast of Hirta. It bears the splendid Gaelic name of Gob na h'Airde, rendered lamely in English as The Point of High Ground.

Our expedition was to the termination of the eastern arm of Gleann Mor—The Great Glen. The Tunnel came into being when the sea washed away the softer rocks, namely three dykes of dolerite, to create a playground of the tides. Salt water, entering at each end, fights a pitched battle in the middle, under the unblinking gaze of grey seals.

We began our expedition with a stroll along the Street. In the village, wild iris (flag) was coming into flower in areas where the drainage was impeded. This flower lights up the Scottish islands in summer. On the moorside, heath spotted orchids, in their thousands, stood to attention. Lousewort was represented in red and white forms. Tormentil was here. In the vicinity of a stream, were some June-flowering primroses.

St. Kildan plants are generally small plants; success attends those that keep down their heads and put down long roots, for they will be battered

The kittiwake, a sea-going gull, has a constitution that belies its gentle appearance.

by the wind, nibbled by sheep and drenched by salt spray. Some coastal areas of Hirta are colonised by grass, plantain and sea-pink, which are among the few plants that survive an onslaught by wind and wave.

An Army landing craft, with fresh supplies, arrived on the high tide and slurred on to the one sandy beach—a beach which is present only in spring and summer. In winter, the searching tides disperse the sand in deeper water. The mouth of the enormous craft opened and soon vehicles were running hither and thither, their drivers anxious that the work should be done before the next tide allowed the landing craft to be backed into the Bay.

All this activity disturbed the kittiwakes that had been washing salt from their feathers in a freshwater pool near the helicopter pad. The half dozen turnstones—wading birds marked like tortoiseshell kittens—continued to feed where the pool emptied into a clear stream.

Our feet encountered the road built for the Army to connect the base with hilltop installations. Near a quarry where fulmars adorned the ledges, and punctuated the long day with their frog-like croaking, stood the Milking Stone. Did the women rest here on their way to and from Glean Mor, in summer, to milk the kine? Did they transport their milk in back-cans—or lock it up as cheese? The Milking Stone is so named because, on specific Sundays, up to about 1764, milk was spilt here to placate a being called Gruagach.

We were tempted on to Mullach Sgar so that we might have a view of The Village. It is an astonishing view of rounded hills, bearing a stubble of short ling, with—low down, near the Bay—a crescent of yellowy-green behind a grey wall and on the green a pattern created by roofless cottages and the innumerable cleits, with a prominent circle representing the wall around the Burial Ground. More stone rings, on the way to the Gap, were built, not to restrain stock, but to keep it away from the ground that was needed for crops.

Nearly every yard of Hirta was being mown finely by the teeth of Soay sheep. The animals left their cast wool—some fawn, some dark brown—as offerings to the earth-god. An ancient writer observed: "There is no sort of Trees, no, not the least Shrub grows here, nor ever a Bee seen at any time."

Having experienced the sublime, we now laughed at the ridiculous. High up, on this island at the edge of the world, where the traffic on a military road consists of one Army vehicle an hour, someone had painted a Zebra Crossing and had reared a Bus Stop and a Pillar Box. The Box, made of concrete and painted bright red, stood near a parting of the ways. We followed the road, passing cleits of the humbler sort. The stones were worn and grey. It was like finding the bleached bones of a herd of animals.

Naturalists visiting Hirta in the spring of 1957 put down traps to catch (alive) any St. Kilda field mice that might have been attracted to the cleits. Mulloch Mor was one of the high-lying, gale-blasted peaks where mice were present in April. The cleits provided the necessary sanctuary. The St. Kilda field mice were at their most concentrated in the vicinity of the Village where, a quarter of a century before, the St. Kilda house mouse had its domain.

Wisps of cloud played hide and seek with each other around the peaks. The hills of Hirta have so little vegetation on them that you feel you can take everything in at a glance. The shapes make a strong appeal and account for their names—Mullach Sgar (Clefted Summit), Mullach Geal (The White top), Mullach Mor (The Big Summit) also the highest of the group, Conachair, the name of which signifies a convergence of the hills.

We were on Mullach Mor, wrapped in cloud. A snipe, startled by a human foot, left its nest. Four eggs were cushioned on vegetation screened by tall grasses. It was tempting to walk further north, hoping to get clear of the cloying vapour. Where the cloud temporarily thinned a great skua—the notorious bonxie—was circling, giving peevish calls. The birds swept down on the boldest member of the party and passed close to his right ear. When the excited skua had landed, someone said: "It reminds me of a big brown hen."

Now we engaged in the ankle-cracking descent of steep ground to the edge of the sea and The Tunnel. A pair of bonxies had young, one of which walked clumsily on its large webbed feet, which looked several sizes too large for the bird!

The Tunnel on the northern shoreline of Hirta is a haunt of Atlantic seals.
Guillemots and kittiwakes nest hereabouts.

A fulmar petrel in flight. The wings are perfectly adapted for long periods of gliding, using the power of the uprising air near the cliffs. St. Kilda held the first British colony of this hitherto far-northern species.

Not only must we cope with the gradient; a half-gale curled over the cliff-edges, knocking us sideways. Astonishingly, fulmars succeeded in hanging in the air, their webbed feet dangling, making subtle adjustments to wing and tail feathers to maintain an equilibirium. In such conditions, I would have expected such a bird to be blown high above the island or, indeed, to be turned inside out!

St. Kilda, with its awesome cliffs, has long appealed to the fulmar. The ancestors of the present birds are believed to have come from Iceland, which was also the source of fulmars found nesting in the Shetland group in the 1870s, much later than the date when nesting began on St. Kilda.

James Fisher, the author of a monograph about the species, and also a frequent visitor to St. Kilda, estimated that at the time of the Evacuation of the people in 1930, some 30,000 pairs of fulmars bred here. The estimated population on the archipelago is now about 44,000 pairs. Almost half of them nest on Hirta.

Fulmars glide on narrow, stiff wings that might be made of balsa wood. They peer at visitors with undisguised interest. Their proneness to spit oil at intruders gives them a somewhat evil reputation. On St. Kilda, where there are far more sheep than humans, the fulmars seem quite timid, being quick to vacate their eggs. A bird that loses its egg does not lay again that year.

A fulmar matures slowly, over some seven years. The breeding season is protracted, from the selection of a nest site early in the year through seven weeks of incubation of the egg, followed by a further seven weeks of the fledgling period. The fulmar normally has a long life, so the population has a sure foundation.

Young fulmars leaving St. Kilda allow the wind to carry them over vast areas of ocean, some reaching Newfoundland, others taking a southward course to Biscay. The older birds remain near the home cliffs, from which they are absent for only a few weeks in the year.

From near the eastern side of The Tunnel, Boreray and the Stacs almost screamed to be photographed and in their grandeur resembled pieces of stage scenery. I shuddered at the sight of members of our party walking on the cliffs. Their diminutive forms looked so vulnerable when set against the sheer rock faces.

Here was St. Kilda at its most magnificent. A sea of Prussian Blue, fringed with white, spent itself against stack and headland. The Boreray group of rocks lay between blue sea and blue sky. Gannets were aloft, heading for the fishing grounds. Kittiwakes had plastered their nests on what looked like impossibly short protruberances from the cliffs. I saw a ledge or two of guillemots. The surface of the sea was broken by the heads of inquisitive grey seals—heads that resembled shiny footballs. The seals stared fixedly at us as they "treaded" water.

Ron walked boldly towards the edge of a cliff. He seemed intent on luring us to our doom. Then we saw the start of a natural ramp leading to the sea—and to the yawning western mouth of The Tunnel. Nature had provided us with a convenient and safe approach.

We descended in bright sunlight, passing tufts of thrift at their summer best. Near The Tunnel, kittiwakes brooded their eggs and had noisy reunions with their mates. Guillemots clung to sloping rock with the desperation of passengers on the deck of a sinking liner.

Gannets were plunge-diving in Glen Bay; we could see the plumes of spray as they hit the water. The sea put on its own show, with surf spreading over the rocks like spilt milk. Yet it was The Tunnel that compelled attention—an enormous hole, sucked smooth. The lowest rocks had been left in a slippery state by the restless tide. We measured our progress in feet per minute. The grey seals watched every footfall. When we had walked as far as we could, we used the eastern end of The Tunnel as a frame when photographing Boreray.

So powerful were the sun's rays that I expected to be able to see the grass of Gleann Mor growing. Bonxies circled and called. Sheep applied themselves vigorously to feeding. From across the Glen came the rowdy voices of lesser black-backed and herring gulls, which are comparative newcomers.

Wiliamson and Boyd, in the delightful book *St. Kilda Summer,* mention that activities springing from the RAF occupation in 1957 materially altered the status of the herring gull at St. Kilda. "Many birds travelled there with the ship which put us ashore on April 16th, but the hundred or so in Village Bay decreased to about thirty when the ship left two days later. However, the next ship, on April 25th, and others between May 1st and 6th, brought fresh arrivals from the Outer Hebrides and most of these elected to stay behind, so that by mid-May we had a village gull-population of over three hundred birds...

The great black-backed gull. It preys on seabirds, especially puffins.

"The gulls remained at this strength until the severe gales of August 23rd-25th, when a steady decline—which kept pace with the withdrawal of the Task Force—began, so that by mid-September only fifty or sixty remained." Gleann Mor had two colonies of lesser blackbacks in 1957.

The Great Glen! The name seems inappropriate to a feature on a speck of rock 100 miles off the Scottish mainland. Nonetheless, the valley we followed was big, broad and in its lushness more like a prairie than a Scottish glen. The Soay sheep had created a pattern of thin trods. Elsewhere, the Great Glen was under-trodden. In our steady ascent we came under the gaze of sheep and gulls and bonxies.

Everywhere was the feeling that some person or persons had been there before us. Quite apart from the tradition of villagers summering their

73

beasts in the Great Glen, and milking the kine here, the human connection was evident in the remains of ancient dwellings.

Ron first showed us the Well of Virtues, with its clear, cool water (the well is said to deliver beer on alternate days!). Martin Martin considered it was the "finest of the excellent fountains or springs in which St. Kilda abounds."

We then examined the traces of early structures, notably the Amazon's House. Archaeologists have scratched and scraped on Hirta. If the earliest people to reach the Hebrides visited St. Kilda, traces of them have not been found. The Neolithic and Mesolithic folk would undoubtedly *see* the islands, blue-grey in the distance when viewed from Harris.

Surely, over a period of several thousand years, little groups of adventurous hunter-gatherers would make the crossing to St. Kilda during the short but bright northern summer and be rewarded by a gargantuan feast of seabirds and their eggs.

Back at the Street, I resumed my visits to the varied stone structures, being scolded by wrens and starlings. Robert Atkinson, in 1938, found piles of fulmars' feathers in many of the byres, which prior to the building of the latest houses had been the homes of the St. Kildans. Even after eight years, those piles of feathers kept their fulmar smell.

At 10pm, the mouse-watchers gathered. Linda, the cook, was tolerant when we put down some biscuit to entice the mice into close range. As she said: "We might as well have the mice on our side. Otherwise they'll be our enemies!"

Ron said he had his own mouse deterrent—a boot, size 9!

Traps used by Robert Atkinson and his friends to catch specimens of the St. Kilda field mouse.

Studies of fowlers by Heathcote and Sands.

First Catch Your Seabird

AS I LAY in bed, reflecting on the day's events, the picture that came repeatedly to mind was that of Boreray and the Stacs, framed by The Tunnel. At 4 am, keen to see Boreray again, I followed the sheep-trods up The Gap to the cliffs that are the seaward termination of Oiseval.

In due course, the sun rose like a fireball, and Boreray and its satellites seemed to glow. Fulmars, gliding by on rigid wings, looked at me with their cold northern eyes. These plunging but well-seamed cliffs of Hirta are perfect nesting places for thousands of fulmars.

I leaned over the cliff. The updraught was tainted with the musky smell of seabirds. Hundreds of fulmars performed a slow ballet in the chilly air; the birds, grey and swirling, gave the impression of a snowstorm that had refused to settle.

I "glassed" the Stacs across four miles of calm water. The big white patches were the nesting areas of gannets. White came partly from their recumbent bodies and partly from the excreta. Three times a year, the men of Hirta crossed the intervening four miles of sea in open boats, their mission being to storm the world's largest nesting place of the North Atlantic gannet for food.

Not that the people were aware of the gannetry's status; it was enough to know that once the difficult landing had been made on rock from a small boat, they might reap a bountiful harvest—eggs, the young, known as gugas, and adults, which impressed by their size, the wings spanning six feet.

In the mid-19th century, attention switched from the gannet to the fulmar. Perhaps the gannet population was on the decline because of over-exploitation. Or the fulmar petrel, here at its only breeding station in Britain, was increasing vastly in number.

The St. Kildans ate fulmar, either fresh or dried; it provided them with valuable protein. The fulmar oil was taken either as a medicine or used in lamps. Fulmar feathers were collected for the factor as a form of rent. Taken to the mainland, they were used for stuffing mattresses—the celebrated "feather bed". (Much better known as a packing is the down taken from the nests of eider ducks).

In a much-quoted passage from the writings of the Rev Kenneth Macaulay, in 1758, the St. Kildan dependence on the fulmar was summarised thus:

"Can the world," said one of the most sensible men on Hirta to me, "exhibit a more valuable commodity? The fulmer (sic) furnishes oil for the lamp, down for the bed, the most salubrious food, and the most efficacious ointments for healing wounds, besides a thousand other virtues of which he is possessed, which I have not time to enumerate. But, to say all in one word, deprive us of the Tulmer, and St. Kilda is no more. . ."

I sat, worshipping the newly-risen sun, on a 550 ft high cliff which was once a workplace for the men of Hirta who, having been lowered over the side on ropes, used their strong nerves and nimble limbs to take the ubiquitous fulmar.

Sometimes, they wore coarse stockings, but mostly they operated with bare feet. Sometimes they climbed without tackle, but mostly they trusted their lives to ropes.

In early times, these ropes were made from strips of cow-hide or from horse-hair. Then came the hempen rope, which must be kept dry when not in use, or it would suffer from fungal infection and be weakened. A cleit, which was dry and airy, made an ideal storage place for the ropes in winter.

Above left: A St. Kildan. *Right and bottom left:* Studies of fowling made by J. Sands. *Bottom right:* A St. Kildan woman with a bundle of freshly-killed fulmars, 1929.

The St. Kildans knew the cliff faces as well as they knew the plots of ground they cultivated at home. Catching seabirds was a vital harvest. Martin Martin recorded that a three-year-old lad was encouraged to climb the drystone walls of a blackhouse to build up his strength and confidence.

Men like Finlay MacQueen became renowned for their athletic exploits on an awe-inspiring cliffscape. Robert Atkinson, who met the ageing Finlay on Hirta in the summer of 1938, recorded that he was still quite insensitive to heights. "He perched on the Lover's Stone, a slice of rock sticking up into thin air from the cliff top. He liked to roll boulders over the edge and watch their frightful plunge and bounce."

There was no need for the old chap to seek birds, but old customs die hard. The two men, St. Kildan and visitor, went to Carn Mor, on the western cliffs, where Finlay prepared his fowling rod, a long tapering pole with a curve of bamboo lashed to the thin end, carrying a running noose made of horse-hair, with a split gannet's quill plaited in to stiffen it.

"The noose hung with hardly a quiver in front of a puffin's breast, then—flip—one bird was struggling wildly and the rest were off in a panic. A pretty skill. Finlay playfully advanced his first puffin to the seat of my trousers, so I was pleased when it turned and got a good hold on the back of his hand and drew blood."

Richard Kearton, impressed by what he considered to be the abnormal size of the ankle joints and the thickness of the insteps of the St. Kildan—a size "brought about, no doubt, by long generations of rock and steep-hill climbing"—arranged for a close-up photograph to be taken of the foot of the native and one of his own feet for comparison!

St. Kildan women were endowed with strong ankles, though a writer was unkind when he compared the ankles and feet of one lady to those of a rhinoceros. A visitor described how young women went with the fowlers to Conachair; the women collected and carried up the easier slopes, thence to the village, any fat young fulmars that were caught. A woman was recorded as carrying a load of birds weighing 200 lb.

At the start of the fowling season, the Village "Parliament" inspected the long ropes and allocated stretches of cliff to the men, who usually worked in pairs, one man remaining on the clifftop and holding the rope, the other end of which was firmly tied around the body, under the arms, of his companion, who might then move about the ledges with confidence.

Part of the technique, when the noose was round a fulmar's neck, and the bird (naturally) began to flap, would be to twist its neck and tie up the beak to retain within the bird's body the oil that had so many uses on the island.

The major expeditions, to Boreray and the Stacs, demanded a large boat and plenty of willing helpers. Martin Martin, accompanying men to

Stac on Armin, saw "a prodigious number of solen geese [gannets] hatching in their nests; the Heavens were darkened by those flying above our heads; their excrements were in such quantity, that they gave a tincture to the sea, and at the same time sullied our boat and clothes."

He was doubtless exaggerating but the Stacs were made for superlatives. The mission awaited settled weather conditions, for an open boat was taken across four and a-half miles of the open Atlantic. Dr MacDonald (1823) was present on Hirta in September, 1822, when boats with loads of young solans were brought home. The tally was 1,600, but 400 had been left on the Stacs for later collection. "When the booty was brought ashore, it was immediately divided, by law, into 120 equal parts, according to the number of the families."

For the first gannet-hunting expedition of the year, a moonless night with a calm sea were the essential requirements. Buchanan recorded what surely is a fanciful account of such an expedition that took place in 1793. A fowler, lowered by rope, silenced the sentinel bird. As he approached it, a cry of *bir, bir* meant alarm, and he would stand back. If the bird cried *grog grog,* he could advance, the bird having taken him to be a late arrival at the rock.

"Then the fowler very gently tickles one of his legs which he lifts and places on the palm of his hand; he then as gently tickles the other, which in like manner is lifted and placed on the hand. He then no less artfully than insensibly moves the sentinel near the first sleeping goose, which he pushes with his fingers; on which he awakes and, finding the sentinel standing above him, he immediately fall a fighting him for his supposed insolence.

"This alarms the whole camp, and instead of flying off they all begin to fight through the whole company; while in the meantime the common enemy, unsuspected, begins in good earnest to twist their necks and never give up till the whole are left dead on the spot."

As dawn came, the bodies of the slain gannets were tossed into the sea, to be collected by the men in the boat.

A trip to Boreray and Stac an Armin in mid-May thinned out the gannet eggs. A gannet that lost its egg would almost certainly lay again. Stac Lee was left alone, to be visited for the young birds.

The Rev Neil Mackenzie wrote in his diary of the fulmar harvest: "The birds must all be caught by hand, and skilfully too, or much of the valuable oil will be lost. They must be caught suddenly and in such a way as to prevent their being able to draw their wings forward or they will squirt the oil. It cannot do this easily while you hold the lower joints of its wings back against each other. Caught in the right way, its neck is speedily twisted and broken and the head passed under the girdle.

"When the man has got strung about him as many as he can conveniently carry, they are passed up to the women who are waiting above. At once they are divided into as many shares as there are men in the group, when the women-kind and children seize upon their shares and begin to drain out the oil into receptacles, which are generally made out of the blown-out and dried stomachs of the Gannet."

A man who watched the cragsmen of St. Kilda from a boat recorded that the minister, Mr McKenzie, gave a pre-arranged signal. "Three or four men, from different parts of the cliff, threw themselves into the air, and darted some distance downwards... They then swung and capered along the face of the precipice, bounding off at intervals by striking their feet against it, and springing from side to side with as much fearless ease and agility as if they were so many schoolboys exercising in a swing a few feet over a soft and balmy clover field. Now they were probably not less than seven hundred feet above the sea..."

On my dawn patrol of the cliffs of Oiseval, the fulmars nested in peace—at least from climbers. The birds had not been harried for 60 years. George Seton, visiting Hirta in July, when the native folks were still in possession, strolled through The Gap to these very cliffs and watched four or five cragsmen set about catching fulmars and puffins.

One man was lowered down the face of the cliff by two of his companions. "Uttering a shrill Gaelic cry, he descended barefooted, skipping and singing as he went, and occasionally standing out nearly at a right angle from the beetling cliff!"

Much has been written of catching seabirds and rather less about how they were dealt with once the share-out had taken place. At home, the St. Kildans gutted and salted the carcasses, which were then kept in barrels (in the cleits) for food. In earlier times, the plucked bodies were simply stored in the cleits; the wind dried the flesh.

The reek of birds and, in the case of fulmars, the reek of oil, impregnated every home. Sands, a visitor to St. Kilda in 1875, reported that 566 gallons of fulmar oil had been collected in a single year. Some of the oil was exported to Skye, where it was used in the smearing of sheep; yet more oil was sold to the Factor.

It was Sands who wrote down, from the dictation of an islander [who surely would find it difficult to keep a straight face] the cries of common St. Kildan seabirds, including:

Gannet: "Gorrok! beero! hurro boo!"
Puffin: "Oh! oh! oh! oh!" (ad infinitum)
Fulmar: "Ok! ok! ok! ok! (allegro)

Fowling on St. Kilda. Finlay MacQueen catching puffins in 1938 (photographed by Robert Atkinson) and in 1896 (a study by Cherry Kearton).

Puffins were snared in large numbers—up to 20,000 puffins a year about 1834, according to a note made by a local minister, the Rev N. MacKenzie. The cull was mainly for the feathers. Snaring puffins was not a pretty sight and, on a remote island, some curious ideas arose, one being the rite of removing, from the first puffin caught, all its feathers except those on the wings and tail. It was set free; then it would be attacked by the other puffins.

Mr Sands saw girls plunging their hands deep into the holes and dragging out the birds. "The necks of the hapless puffins were twisted with a dexterity which only long practice could give." Even dogs were trained to catch puffins.

Among Frank Lowe's effects was a puffin snare he collected on Hirta in 1929. It consists of a length of stout cord, some 44 inches long, with about 30 much thinner lengths of what appear to be two-ply horse hair twisted into the cord. It is possible that the St. Kildans were importing horse hair for this purpose.

Each end of a length of horse hair is knotted and just a few lengths have a loop made in the form of a running noose, except that in this case, it would be devised for capturing a puffin by a leg rather than its neck. Presumably, when the snare was first made, all the pieces of horse hair would have been capable of trapping a puffin. With time, some pieces had become unlooped.

At each end of the cord are small strips of sacking—which would have been readily available, certainly in the late 19th century, when various goods were being brought on to the island. The sacking forms a loop which could then be used with pegs to tether the snare.

From accounts of life on St. Kilda, it would appear that once a single puffin had been trapped by its feet catching in a horse hair noose, and was struggling, other puffins—ever inquisitive—would converge to have a look. So a snare, left out on the cliff edge, might catch several birds at a time.

Macculloch, in an often quoted passage, reflected on the St. Kildan dependence on the seafowl: "The air is full of feathered animals, the sea is covered with them, the houses are ornamented by them, the ground is speckled with them like a flowery meadow in May. The town is paved with feathers, the very dunghills are made of feathers, the plough land seems as it had been sown with feathers, and the inhabitants look as if they had been all tarred and feathered, for their hair is full of feathers, and their clothes are covered with feathers."

Men still talk admiringly of the fowling prowess of Finlay MacQueen. Robert Atkinson, on his visit in 1938, got to know Finlay well. He has provided word pictures of him in later life, providing a contrast with the lively, untiring man of the crags.

"Finlay went his own way; his housekeeping, bird-snaring and crotal hoeing kept him occupied; he leavened these activities with a little daytime sleep and with Bible reading. On a fine day he put out his dried fish to air and to gather the bluebottles, or he looked through his uninviting stock of fulmars—birds snared earlier in the year, plucked, split and preserved in brine."

A prospect of the Cambir and Soay.

A Cliff-top Route to the Cambir

CLIMATICALLY, the liveliest time on Hirta was around dawn. One morning, a heavy shower swept the Village as though someone had decreed the place should be given a good wash at the start of a new day. I heard the rain pouring on to the felt-and-bitumen roof with the intensity of water hurled from a bucket. The wild spell proved to be but a 10-minute interlude in an otherwise calm period of weather.

· Another morning there was a rollocking wind. It stormed the Village, passing our lodgings with a sound like an express train. The bothy door was blown open. I had an earlier-than-usual view of Village Bay.

The young Army captain mentioned the Mudscape he experienced in the first storm-wracked months of his appointment. "Spring came on April 1. That day the first puffin arrived; the first lamb was born and the air temperature became reasonable. . ." He went on to tell of the miseries of being on St. Kilda when the wind speed reached 195 miles an hour, putting the radar out of action and giving everyone a touch of melancholia.

The weather was transient. It was never really bad. For several days the sky was the bluest of blues; then a few clouds were tethered to the highest hills and we had days when mist created a washday atmosphere. I never saw one of those languid skies in which cumulus hang about like giant woolsacks. I did experience evenings of absolute clarity and calmness when the light stonework of Village and cleits was tinted gold by the sun as it quested for the horizon.

We had one truly bad day, when the Weather Clerk served up a mixture of wind, rain and low cloud. Village Bay became a turmoil of spray-crested waves that broke their backs dramatically on the sandy beach. The humidity was such that some of us seriously considered moving into a cleit.

I think it was Myles who suggested a swim. Soon half a dozen people, having donned swimming costumes and raincoats, were dashing through rain to the beach. Coats and footwear were cast and the bathers advanced towards walls of water that came grandly towards them. Both met in a tumult of water and spray and amid shrieks of pleasure from the bathers. It was all very elemental. The bathers had a feeling of achievement, for on that day some of the gulls were grounded!

In terms of art, St. Kilda is best suited to water-colour, which can be applied with brisk washes and strokes. I sketched, using a felt-tipped pen, plus spit and finger-end to create washes. I would spend half an hour before breakfast in the Museum, sketching reminders of the old way of life—a replica of the St. Kilda mailboat and a cracked cooking utensil, a broken bottle and photographic images of long-dead islanders, forever "frozen" in attitudes of daily work by Victorian and Edwardian cameramen.

The St. Kildan day began with the obligatory shower or with mist of such liquid consistency it might almost be drizzle. I was heartened when, sitting up in bed, I saw that sunlight had banded the top of Mullach Sgar. A stray shaft of sunlight brought an amber-like glow to a bottle of whisky someone had left on a window ledge.

It was never dark on Hirta. At midnight, if I crept from my bed to answer a Call of Nature or to visit the night-calling petrels, I could see clearly by the orange glare from the military base. The rhythmic thudding of the generator seemed to make the old rocks quiver.

As I walked along the Street, with a few clothes over my pyjamas and some wellies on my feet, I might see a faint light burning in the kitchen and discover that some of the lads were still yarning, mouse-watching or gloating over codling that had been jerked from the sea just off the Point.

The big wall between the Factor's House and Feather Store, also the boulder slope beyond, were the nursery areas of the storm petrel. This small, dark bird with a prominent white rump spends most of its life far out at sea, but must return to land to nest. It selects burrows or holes in walls and conducts its nesting programme by night, when predatory birds like the big gulls are at rest.

A pair of petrels go through a tender courtship, incubate the egg and feed the young on a shift system, the birds changing over in the blackest part of the night. Strange calls and bat-like forms are to be noted by the nocturnal bird-watcher. The indispensable Robert Atkinson referred to "an astonishing noise...a long, loud churring as of rolled rr's, a frog's noise, but periodically broken off by a sudden exclamation, as if the maker had been overtaken by a hiccup."

When daylight comes, the nesting areas of the storm petrels appear devoid of life.

At sea, I had seen the birds flying close to the boat, presumably to dine on any morsels of food disturbed by the whirring propellers. On Hirta, when the petrel forms were hard to pick out, I could at least recall the characteristic darting flight, and the way a bird's webbed feet dangled.

Storm petrels which nest in quite dense colonies are thinly spread across the sea. The nesting place is constricted; the sea is vast and petrels feed at the limit of the Continental Shelf. Long journeys do not daunt birds that, despite their smallness, winter on the ocean.

Most times, during my visits to the high wall, I heard only the chickering calls in the darkness. I pressed an ear against a crack between smooth, rounded stones and heard the harsh uneven purring—urr-r-r-r-r—and the sudden hiccough, which one imaginative ornithologist likened to "a fairy being sick."

Hirta teems with storm petrels. In 1978, naturalists with mist-nets trapped, ringed and released over 2,000 adults which had their nests under the rocks behind the Factor's House.

After my close encounter with petrels, I would sneak back to bed and, a few hours later, greet a new day by going for a shower, nodding at the singing wrens and the highly-strung sheep. As I luxuriated in a flow of hot water I had a view through the window of great hills banded with sunlight.

Ron organised an expedition to The Cambir, on the north-western rim of Hirta. Our undulating course lay along the rim of the magnificent western cliffs. We followed the military road but struck off towards a weathered outcrop nicknamed General de Gaulle because it resembles a head with a prominent nose.

Someone posed on the rim of the Lover's Stone, or what is now called the Lover's Stone. Anyone who has read a popular history of St. Kilda will have become familiar with an ordeal faced by a young St. Kildan male who wished suitably to express the depth of his love for a girl.

The so-called Lover's Stone on Hirta, photographed by Frank Lowe in 1929.

At the Lover's Stone, the young lad must stand on his left foot. I now quote Martin Martin: "Having the one Half of it over the Rock, he then draws the right Foot towards the left, and in this Posture bowing, puts both his Fists further out to the right Foot; after he has performed this, he has acquired no small Reputation, being ever after accounted worthy of the finest Woman in the World."

The story was first told about the Mistress Stone on Ruaival, and that is about a third of a mile from the so-called Lovers' Stone. It was a visitor called Heathcote who confused the matter by drawing the Lovers' Stone for his book, published in 1900. Perhaps he preferred the grander silhouette.

Two members of our party posed on the stone finger of Heathcote's Lover's Stone. One of them reported: "The view's grand".

We stared down, down, down, over boulders and scree and patches of grass to where the sea was smacking its lips against smooth rock. Here at Carn Mor we were at one of the great bird haunts of Hirta. The birds, mainly petrels, were conspicuous by their absence, many of them tucked away among the boulders and many feeding out at sea.

Three species of petrel nest under a jumble of grey rocks, beneath Mullach, the peak of which forms an impressive rock steeple. The ledges of Mullach Bi, like most parts of Hirta, had been colonised by that daytime-flying petrel, the fulmar.

Gwen found a cavity in the rock and impulsively thumped the ground with her boot, bringing a response from a Manx shearwater. More thumps stimulated an unseen bird to make more strange calls. I was amused by the descriptions of those who heard it.

"It sounds like like a cockerel that's being strangled";

"It's like a squeaky toy that's gone wrong", and—

"It's an inhalation, then one, two, three—OUT."

A member of our party who had heard wedge-tailed shearwaters on the Great Barrier Reef insisted on imitating the call they made!

By day, Carn Mor has much to commend it. Thousands of puffins nest hereabouts and in the gloaming their massed flight is spectacular. When the puffins are roosting, and the night-shift takes over, an eerie ballet takes place as Manx shearwaters, Leach's petrels and storm petrels return from the ocean to their nests and, finding them unerringly, change over nesting duties with their mates, which have been incubating the eggs or brooding the chicks.

All this happens at the darkest part of the night. The human watcher is aware of a flicker of wings and, most of all, of the strange calls of the ocean-going birds. He or she may unknowingly be sitting at the entrance to a petrel's burrow. Suddenly, a bird plops down and demands an entry.

When the sky pearls at the approach of dawn, Carn Mor is once again as quiet as a graveyard.

We scrambled over the topmost rocks of Mullach Bi. Now our feet were rustling against the broad, dry leaves of woodrush. Elsewhere, the ground was spangled with celandines and mouse-eared chickweed.

Every view from a cliff edge was spectacular, with steep cliffs and steep grassy slopes, the haunt of fulmars, puffins and the lithesome Soay sheep. I recall in particular the fulmars. There were so many of them. They occupied every suitable ledge and "pockets" in the vegetational cover. In every seaward view, scores of fulmars hung on the wind. It was like a display of feathered kites.

A fulmar petrel on its nesting ledge.

We passed some natural gardens—cushions of sea pink, grouped in the lee of rocks, one group having double beauty by being reflected in a still pool. We ran the gauntlet of some squawking gulls, and were dived upon by the ubiquitous bonxie, protecting its young. The bonxie's approach was a shallow dive. There was plenty of time to locate it and to appreciate its intentions before it was darting by, at a range of a few inches, with a whoosh of displaced air.

Meanwhile, the mate was lining up to continue the harassment.

The Cambir is like a clenched fist in the north-western corner of Hirta. Its summit is almost 700 feet above where the waves break grandly against dark rock. But when approached from the south, The Cambir loses out to the island of Soay, which looms beyond. The gap between them is not visible from this direction.

We were aware at the final approach of a being on a neck of soft rock which was being eroded to create an island from The Cambir. In due course, the island would become a stack, then a skerry, then just a patch of white water to be seen against the racing tide.

Far below, among the wild waves, grey seals had hauled themselves on to a flat slab of rock and were basking in the summer sunshine. From a distance, the bodies in repose were like enormous slugs.

At the rocky rim of The Cambir, rain fell in a short, sharp shower from an otherwise clear sky. We saw more windborne fulmars. Stacs and skerries lay between Hirta and Soay, the sheep island. This not inconsiderable island of 250 acres has a maximum height of 1,225 feet. Basically, Soay is a block of gabbro thatched with soil and grass that is kept lush by the grazing primitive sheep and the droppings of numerous seabirds. Soay is also the westernmost island of Scotland.

In 1856, families living on Hirta gave up the unequal struggle with a hard landscape and the elements and went off to Australia, selling their stock of sheep on Soay to the Laird, who was content to leave the place as it was. And so it remained while elsewhere in the Hebrides the native sheep breed was being improved by the introduction of Blackface and Cheviot.

Several times a year, the men of Hirta crossed the sound of Soay to cull the sheep. It is related that the dogs had their teeth filed smooth so they would not cause excessive injury to the sheep. Maybe a score of sheep were caught. There followed the difficult task of transporting them—two sheep a man—down a steep cliff to the boat.

Mary Harman explained to us how she hoped to land on Soay from a boat and climb to a place where she might pitch a tent. She would stay for a week, recording the archaeological remains. Two bird-watchers would also be landed, their mission being to count seabirds.

A Soay sheep, looking dishevelled because it is in the moult.

The Kearton brothers found "Soa" the most awkward island of the group on which to effect a landing. "We got ashore, after a great deal of scrambling and excitement, at a place where the rocks sloped at a much more acute angle than the roof of most houses, and were in addition covered by a crop of extremely slippery sea-weed. From this point we were all tied together, Alpine fashion, and began to ascent the almost perpendicular cliff by the aid of crannies and ledges, which were in many places not more than an inch in depth, and barely afforded a sufficient resting-place for our toes or finger-tips.

"On arriving at a place where the precipice was broken up into huge boulders and shelves which admitted of easier and safer progress, the men began to give us an exhibition of their skill with the fowling-rod amongst the Guillemots and Razorbills. Some of their captures were so clever that it appeared as if they exercised some kind of destructive charm over the poor birds."

We saw the remains of the aircraft of the 1939-45 war. This plane had not quite reached the grassy top of Soay. The pilot's last view would be of banking near the rock pinnacles of Stac na Biorrach and Tac Dona, in the channel. The stubs of ancient rock are forever fringed by milky foam. Historians of the sport of climbing are fond of quoting from Sir Robert Moray, who in 1698 described a climb of Stac na Biorrach. His account, which is said to be the first for any climb in Britain, must have been based on observing a fowling group.

Sir Robert landed at a place where he had room for but one of his feet. The visiting climber had to ascend 12 or 16 fathoms. "Then he comes to a place where, having but room for his left foot and left hand, he must leap from thence to another place before him, which if he hit right the rest of the ascent is easy, and with a small cord which he carried with him he hales up a rope whereby all the rest come up.

"But if he misseth that footstep (as often times they do) he falls into the sea, and the company takes him in by the small cord and he sits still until he is a little refreshed and then he tries it again; for everyone there is not able for that sport."

We again ran the gauntlet of the bonxies.

We heard the dolorous voices of big gulls from an area where their nests were widespread between the rocks, the vegetation having been padded flat and lifeless by many webbed feet.

Across the Bay, and the mouth of the north glen, lay the headland pierced by the famous Tunnel. Our eyes located the down-tilted sill we had used to reach the Tunnel. So neat did the sill appear, it might have been blasted from the living rock for the convenience of visitors.

The Rock Wall of Conachair

A ST. KILDAN DAY was not complete without a walk from the Village to Look-out Gap, between Oiseval and Conachair. The exercise was not strenuous, being on an easy gradient. From the edge of Village Bay the path rose for a mere 500 feet to the island's eastern rim and the astonishing view of Boreray.

Turn left at the Gap, and the walk might be extended to the grassy summit of Conachair—to this breezy summit of Hirta. Conachair turns a sheer granite face to the ocean. Its awesome sea cliff is, at 1,397 feet, the highest in Britain, being fractionally higher than the Kame on Foula, the westernmost of the Shetland group.

Julian Huxley noted: "The entire slope is dotted with white specks. The impression is of strange cliff flowers; but they are in reality fulmars." The air holds more fulmars. They ride the uprush of air with scarcely a beat of their wings. They come close, to survey the visitor intently. They are silent, these grey ghosts of the northern sea that come to places like Hirta for a protracted nesting programme.

I first saw the cliff of Conachair under a cloudless sky. St. Kilda often frustrates the visitor with its cloud and mist. The island group is a great manufacturer of clouds. Martin Martin, the 17th century visitor, noted:

"The Hills are often covered with ambient White Mists. . . in Summer, if only on the Tops of the Hills, they prognosticate Rain; and when they descend to the Valleys it is a Prognostick of excessive Heat."

The first time I went to Conachair, it was as a member of a small group led by Ron, who used Boreray and the Stacs as markers for a glimpse of land on the horizon. In clear view were three of the Seven Hunters—otherwise known as the Flannan Islands. The loom of the Flannan light is visible on Hirta in clear weather.

The Flannans, like St. Kilda, are remnants of an ancient landscape, now stubbornly resisting the worst that the weather and the Atlantic can do. The Hebridean outliers include Rona, 44 miles to the north of the Butt of Lewis, which is named after the grey seals that drop their pups here, and Sula Sgeir, a remote rock taking its name from the nesting gannets. For many years, men from Lewis made a hazardous sea crossing to Sula Sgeir in September to harvest the young birds as food; they still have the right to do this but they exercise it in larger motor craft.

Presiding over the scattering of islands known as the Flannans is Eileen Mor, with its remains of the 8th century chapel of St. Flannan and a lighthouse built in 1899 by the Stevensons of Edinburgh, a family from which sprang Robert Louis Stevenson, the author of *Treasure Island*. The Flannans have a mystery similar to that of the "Marie Celeste", though in this case the lighthousemen were missing without trace. The captain of a passing steamer reported that the light was out. The Northern Lighthouse Board investigated and a landing party found a deserted lighthouse. A meal of cold meat, pickles and potatoes for three lay on the table; one chair had been knocked over. The last entry in the logbook was for a day of wild weather.

It is theorised that two of the party went to investigate damage; the third, rushing after them when he noticed the conditions deteriorating, was close by when all three were swept into the sea.

Ron led us to what is romantically known as The Cleit at the Edge of the World. Like much else on Hirta, it appeared as part of a surprise view. Having reached what appeared to be a cliff edge, Ron invited us to look over it. The ground was steep but not sheer and we negotiated it to reach a grassy ledge on which stood the little cleit. The stones gleamed so brightly in the afternoon sunshine that each stone might have had its own power source.

The granite wall of Conachair was awesome in its immensity. Even a wide-angle lens could not satisfactorily cope with its height of a quarter of a mile. I saw grassy slopes, areas of naked rock, more grass, then bare cliffs and sea caves, with two splendid stacs and skerries being washed by a gentle sea.

Round a corner, and in the shadows, were nesting fulmars, two of which spat at me. Fulmars were in possession of the main cliff. They had little to say to us, but stared unblinking and periodically shuffled to turn the eggs beneath them.

Our walk continued with a climb to the summit of Conachair, passing some remnants of a Beaufighter aircraft of the 1939-45 war. I touched a twisted propeller. The Beaufighter spirit lives on in the great skua—the notorious bonxie—which at that moment decided on a power dive to within an inch or two of my unprotected head.

Grass and heather extended to the summit of the hill. Where the bare bones of the landscape struck through, we were looking at a cream-coloured granite, smoothed by the Atlantic weather.

The way down was unrelentingly steep. The only horizontal objects were the roofs of some of the cleits I passed, slowly, in deference to the welfare of my ankles. The geriatrics took their time; the most active were down in the Village and resuming work on the roof of No.1 Cottage long before we had come to the Boundary Wall that signified the edge of the wilderness.

I did stop now and again to admire the view, and not for the usual reason: that I wanted a rest. The almost theatrical appearance of Village Bay and the strange, serrated outline of Dun, like some prehistoric lizard, deserved attention. As the swell broke, it formed a white frill at the edge of Dun which, like St. Kilda as a whole, is being salt-licked into oblivion.

A supply ship in Village Bay.

Later, standing beside a cleit so as to be inconspicious, I watched a group of St. Kilda's distinctive sheep, which have been described as living fossils. Since they were introduced by the Norse folk—for so it is presumed—they do not appear to have been crossed with any other breed. If this is true, we are looking at what resembles the domestic sheep of a millennium ago.

The St. Kildans were sometimes capable of running down and catching a nimble Soay sheep. Martin Martin relates:

"There are none to catch them but the Inhabitants, whom I have seen pursue the Sheep nimbly down the steep descent, with as great freedom as if it had been a plain Field."

As already related, their purity of breed was ensured by the survival of a group on the island of Soay; hence a common name for the breed—Soay sheep. Even when people lived on Hirta, with their cattle and improved breeds of sheep, the old type persisted on Soay, being the property of the laird—the McLeod of McLeod.

The factor of St. Kilda told the Kearton brothers in 1896 that McLeod had objected when the men of Hirta wanted to cross Soay sheep with their blackfaced breed. MacLeod had taken over the island of Soay and its sheep. He thereafter charged the natives 2s. 6d for every sheep they caught there.

Several years after the Evacuation of Hirta, the blackfaced type of sheep that had escaped the round-up were taken away; the new laird, the Marquis of Bute, had some of the old type brought over from Soay. They were the ancestors of those that live in a wild state today. (The last of the blackfaced sheep, on Boreray, must be counted half-wild, since they have not been shepherded for 60 years).

The old breed of sheep, now the most primitive sheep in Europe, follow the ancient rituals of the breed. By October, the rams are intolerant of each other. The mating season is at hand. Rivals meet head to head with a dull "clunk". If any creature knows the miseries of headache, it must be a Soay sheep at mating time. Rams also "block" each other, walking side by side, with one attempting to turn the other away from the ewes.

The sheep tend to disperse for lambing. The student of sheep told me that an enemy of the lambs is the great black backed gull. It has the noxious habit of penetrating the rectum of a lamb, which is then deftly turned inside out.

The chief enemy of a sheep is—another sheep! Because they are not culled, as are domesticated breeds of sheep, the population rises from around 600 to nearly three times that figure—to a level at which there is overgrazing, which leads to malnutrition, and a heavy burden of parasites. The result is what biologists call a "crash".

Soay sheep are long-lived, up to 10 years, so the population decline is not disastrous. The survivors have some good years of breeding ahead of them. Precocious lambs are receptive to the tup before they are 12 months old. Happily, these island sheep do not suffer from a strike by fly. If you find yourself itching after forty winks on the Hirta sheep range, you will have attracted a ked or a louse!

The Church was a place to visit for a quiet moment. A large window in the gable end fed the summer light on to the rostrum in the huge pulpit. On the rostrum lay a large copy of the Authorised Version of the Bible. The organ was small and modern. The summer light brought a gleam to brass plaques on the cream upper walls; lower down the colour was brown.

I envied Robert Atkinson his experience of St. Kildan form of worship, as practised by three elderly St. Kildans, on a summer visit to their native island in 1938. Each Sabbath morning and evening, in Sunday best, they walked slowly past the factor's house on their way to the "dust-deep" church.

"I cleared a space in the debris of a seat at the back and sat down. Finlay (MacQueen) in spectacles conducted the service: prayers, psalms read and then sung, Bible reading, a twenty-minute sermon. They all sang the psalms in a soaring and swooping dirge, often nasally out of tune or out of time with each other, but they made a loud unselfconscious noise. The prayers were said fervently in an almost agonised hoarse whisper. Finlay's sermon echoed round the room . . .

Church treasures removed from the Church in 1930 for safe-keeping in Edinburgh.

A Free Church Minister.

"The large dirty room and the congregation of three—or four—put a strangeness on the performance which the St. Kildans evidently did not feel: and why indeed should they!... "They had been reared from birth to this religion so it came as naturally and essentially to them as eating or drinking (though it was a little odd that they didn't clear up their sacred house)."

Only 40 years previously, when the Keartons went to that self-same church, the floor, except the sections just beneath the feet of the worshippers, "consists entirely of Mother Earth". The minister himself had laid cement in the aisle. The cement was given by a generous donor, and when the "bags of dust" arrived on the steamer no one on the island was quite sure what to do with them. They put them outside the church and, by the following summer, when a visitor inquired about them, the dust had miraculously turned into "rock".

The Keartons, coming from the Yorkshire Dales, where a Sabbatical hush descended on one day in seven, arose early on the first Sunday they spent on Hirta. They hung about until 11 a.m. without seeing anyone "on devotions bent".

At 12.30 p.m., worshippers were summoned to the kirk by the ringing of an old ship's bell. Then they heard that the minister, Mr. Fiddes, had given his little flock an hour and a half's grace "out of compassion for them, on account of their extra toil and exertion in landing their provisions the previous day."

The service was in Gaelic, the sermon lasted one and a-half hours, and after the service the women left the church before the men moved at all. "I was greatly pleased with this custom, thinking it to be a courteous deference shown to the fair sex of St. Kilda, whose industry and modesty render them entirely worthy of it, but have since learnt that it is a lingering relic of Roman Catholicism which is still in force on the Continent."

And this was the kirk where, in the stern old days of the 1870s, it was reported that the people went to church "with sorrowful looks, and eyes bent upon the ground like a troop of the damned being driven by Satan to the bottomless pit."

It sounds as though another visitor to St. Kilda was making yet another snap-decision about the local way of life.

Women and children on Hirta, 1929.

GEMINI INFLATABLE CRAFT FERRYING MATERIAL FROM
SHIP TO SHORE IN VILLAGE BAY, HIRTA.

By Gemini to Dún

THE ARMY delivered us to the island of Dun. An immense fork-lift truck picked up a Gemini inflatable and lumbered with it to the sea, placing it gently on the water. We were taken, three or four at a time, from the side of the pier to where a thick white rope extended down the rocks to the western edge of Village Bay.

While waiting to board the craft, I watched a peregrine in rapid flight across the top of Oiseval. House martins and swallows had arrived from— who knows where? They do not normally nest on Hirta and it was now mid-June. A gannet dived in the Bay and its manner on surfacing suggested that it had caught a fish, possibly a saithe. Mackerel was once an important prey item.

Our Gemini left a bubbling wake as we went "wave-bashing", to quote the soldier in charge. That morning, there were few waves to bash and, most significantly, no line of white water along the rim of Dun.

The soldier, a young lad from the West Country, first directed the Gemini to where a million tides had eroded a tunnel through rock. This was on the Hirta side of the 50 yard wide Sound that is to Dun what a moat is to a castle. The comparison is apt. Dun is a Celtic word, meaning a fort.

At the approaches to the Cave we were instructed to lean to the right, for the roof sloped steeply. Our Gemini briefly left the daylight and the excited kittiwakes for calm water that had the colour of jade. We emerged into the approach to Dun Narrows with a view of the Dun cliff, rimmed by nesting fulmars and pouting puffins. A few pairs of black guillemots are to be found in the gap.

On our approach to the shore of Dun—and to the white rope—we were welcomed by an eider duck that had a black-downed youngster riding on its back.

The Keartons were rowed to Dun by a party who included Finlay Mac-Queen. The brothers had first visited Dun Sound to take photographs. "We found it impossible to make a picture on account of the showers of fine spray which were being driven through the defile, blurring the lens of our camera the moment it was exposed."

They returned to the boat with difficulty. "It was jigging about like a cork in a whirlpool on account of a heavy ground swell and the rush of a current which came from a cave close by."

Our party landed near the inlet known as Seilg Geo. The Bay had looked calm but was experiencing a slight swell. Water sploshed against the smooth rocks. The rope was long enough to be held when the boat was riding high. It slipped from the grasp as the boat fell back.

We grasped the rope in turn, some showing confidence, others desperation. Some remained dryshod and others had their footwear filled with water. When there was time to look around, we found ourselves in a natural garden. From cracks in the volcanic rocks—rocks that that had a dull red appearance and might have set in terror—grew a miscellany of salt-tolerant plants, including thrift and white campion. Higher up, an eider sat impassively on its down-lagged nest.

The usual reception committee was there: fulmars, some of them in pairs, uttering their dry croaks.

Dun, a mile long rocky ridge, attains its summit at Bioda Mor. Dun has for long given protection to Village Bay and Hirta but has suffered in consequence. When the sea has a storm-force wind behind it, sheets of spray overtop the island and pour like torrential rain into Village Bay. The southern rocks are grey and seamed, like the skin of a reptile.

Fulmar

The fulmar. *Above:* A photograph taken on Hirta. *Right:* The drawing of a fulmar in Martin Martin's book of 1698 clearly shows the bird's tubed beak.

A Pouting Puffin!

Dun welcomes seabirds. It has ledges, stacks, peaty areas and boulder slopes to appeal to most maritime species. In spring and early summer it becomes a gigantic bird nursery. Every niche on the long narrow ridge appears to be used for nesting.

The sharp crest of the island divides the southern side, where the cliffs are up to 500 feet high, from the northern side, an area of steeply shelving slopes, riddled with puffin burrows. Dun has a community of St. Kilda (long-tailed) mice but, happily for the vulnerable nesting birds, no rats.

We advanced through an area where sheep have been absent for many years. Plants have grown vigorously, and in some areas had been nourished by tons of guano from the massed bird life. Common sorrel had formed a mini-jungle. Lesser celandine was common. Scentless mayweed, coming into flower, appeared in every view. We saw the dead stalks of angelica.

Old puffin areas were still spongy; those in current use showed exposed earth that had been pounded flat by webbed feet. It was wise to ignore such areas or a thoughtlessly placed foot would go through the roof of a puffin burrow.

"Puffin vegetation" was mentioned in the latest guide book to St. Kilda. The plant communities have been greatly modified by the manurial, burrowing and trampling effects of birds, mainly puffins. Sheep's sorrel is the dominant plant. Also represented in these areas are Yorkshire fog and plants to which reference has already been made.

Dun would be a relatively quiet island but for the noisy incomers of

St. Kilda wren, photographed by
Robert Atkinson in 1938.

recent years. I refer to the gulls. Lesser blackbacks and herring gulls circled
and screamed abuse. I heard a bass-baritone voice from a great black-
backed gull, a maritime bully-boy. Several pairs of great blackbacks were
nesting on Dun.

St. Kilda wrens were in profusion; the voices of the cock birds sounded
above all other sounds. It astonished me, while sitting on the crest of the
island, with seabirds all around, to hear a cascade of sharp, clear notes
from a cock wren and to find the wren perched on a lichen-encrusted
boulder, within a few feet of a puffin or a fulmar.

Puffins were common, but we were in an area of light to medium col-
onisation; the heaviest concentration was towards the tip of Dun. (At St.
Kilda, the puffin population can be divided into three, with a third each on
Dun, Boreray and Soay). Fulmars and puffins appear to co-exist well.

We walked to the limit of the permitted area, beyond which puffins filled the air with the density of bees around a hive. Village Bay was speckled
with off-duty birds. I watched a puffin from close range as it posed on a
rock festooned with orange lichen. From the puffin's parrot-like beak were
draped half a dozen sand-eels: silvery fish that gleamed in the bright light.

There is no precise figure for Dun's puffin population, but it is
somewhere between 60,000 and 80,000 pairs. The numbers are at a lower
level than previously. The northern seas are being denuded of their fish,
and the puffin is partial to the sand-eel, which is now being sought
commercially.

The fulmar is locally common, with some 7,000 pairs. It was on Dun
that Finlay MacQueen and a companion, Finlay Gillies, demonstrated their
skill with the fowling rod to the Kearton brothers.

Frank Lowe's study of seabirds on St. Kilda, 1929.

Finlay MacQueen had a rope tied round his waist for safety and then he crept down a rope, rod in hand, until he was within range of fulmars. Quietly, he pushed the rod forward until the open noose at the end dangled just before the head of his victim; then, by a dexterous twist of the wrist, he slipped the noose round the luckless bird's neck. In its struggles, the fulmar succeeded only in tightening the noose.

The sea roared into geo's and thundered against volcanic walls the sea's violence had already converted into overhangs; here and there it surged through arches. Kittiwakes had plastered their nests against the merest knobs of rock in shallow caves. Guillemot ledges were noticeable because of the well-spread guano. I did not see many guillemots. About 1,000 pairs of razorbills nest between the volcanic rocks of Dun.

The puffins fascinated us by their appearance and behaviour. One of our little group said: "It's nice to watch another species that doesn't feel it has to be working all day long. The puffins don't seem to do anything." So I watched a group of puffins. They *were* busy—in their way. One puffin stretched its wings after landing and used the wings to assist its progress up a shallow slope. I was reminded of film I had seen of penguins coming ashore in the Antarctic.

Another puffin was preening systematically. A gossiping group had formed at the cliffe edge. None of the birds seemed to move, but when I watched with special care, they were shuffling about. Their positions changed—by the minute.

Whether in flight or on the ground, puffins were forever looking over their shoulders, as well they might. The great blackbacks dine on puffins. The few local pairs of gulls are believed to take over 2,000 puffins in the nesting season. They deftly turn a body inside out to expose the flesh.

Puffins that alighted with sand-eels dangling from their huge, laterally flattened beaks had special reason to go to earth quickly, before they could be mugged by the larger birds.

In August, the young puffins depart from Dun by night, to avoid being attacked by the big gulls, which are then roosting. The juvenile puffins are seen at the mouth of the burrows; they exercise their wings. The puffin chick is fed by its parents until it is ready to leave. A fall-off in weight towards the end of the landbound period, once interpreted as "starving", is now believed to represent the conversion of fat.

The young birds walk or fly to the sea. Light attracts them. On Hirta, at the time when young puffins are leaving, the outside lights of the Army complex are switched off. Even so, it has been known for up to 200 puffin chicks to land on the Hirta shore in a single night; they are collected, have light alloy rings attached to their legs and are released next day.

We had our movements restricted by the needs of conservation. One could imagine the grandeur of the southern tip of the island, where a wall has been associated with the notion that a fort once stood at the tip of the island. Britain's largest colony of Leach's petrel is to be found near the tip of Dun. Here, too, are shags and razorbills in large numbers.

Making a bee-line from the Altar to Selig Geo, I flushed three snipe from a moist area and then began to hear the dry croaks of fulmars from nests among boulders and rank vegetation. A few birds struggled into view with the effect of minor explosions. Some of them spat oil.

The Gemini collected us and resumed its wave-bashing. On the way back to the pier, its ability to manoeuvre was demonstrated. This brought to mind the Kearton story of Finlay MacQueen, the fowler, and his friends. Their large rowing boat had "jigged about like a cork" on the swell.

A few hours later, the Gemini was launched again and its seething wake led the eye directly to a Dutch trawler at the mouth of the Bay. A member of the crew had lacerated a hand, which needed medical attention. He was conveyed to the sick-bay on Hirta.

As this was being carried out, a team representing the National Trust for Scotland was playing an Army team at hockey in the recreation hall. The tallest of the Army players—who wore a T-shirt marked JOGGING KILLS—left his unfinished can of ale on a ledge at a height of about 12 feet. He reached it by leaping up against a wall and using his own great height. No one else could reach that can!

The Army won the match: 16-6.

Dun continued to exert a strong fascination. On my evening walk to Ruaival, I looked across the sound at the massed seabirds. I then climbed to the Mistress Stone. The wind was so strong, I encountered Vertical Take-Off Starlings. Birds that had been feeding young at the nests in the jumble of boulders emerged normally but shot upwards when caught by the furious draught from the cliff.

A group of razorbills on Dun.

A "St. Kilda Mail" of 1938.

Postcards on the Ebb Tide

COTTAGE No. 3 had been converted into a museum. Assembling pictures and artefacts to tell the St. Kilda story had clearly been a job performed by a professional. This museum was graphic, uncluttered—and warm.

Here I came under the beady gaze of a representation of the Garefowl, otherwise known as the Great Auk, a giant razorbill that paddled its way to and fro across the Atlantic from its wintering quarters to its breeding rocks. The cudgels of native folk, of seafarers who were craving for fresh meat and of specimen-hunters anxious to collect skins or eggs, had rendered the Garefowl extinct by 1844.

This flightless auk regularly visited St. Kilda to breed until about the time of Martin Martin's visit in the late 17th century. By the middle of the 18th century there were irregular sightings. Atkinson (1831) wrote of its "coming once in ten or a dozen years and never breeding."

A tale is told that the last Garefowl in Britain died on Stac an Armin about 1840, being slain by two St. Kildans who associated it with witchcraft.

To me, the most fascinating item in the museum was a replica of the St. Kilda Mail—a piece of wood, carved with great simplicity into the shape of a boat, with a length of rope connecting it to a bladder. Anyone who reads about St. Kilda learns about this novel way of communicating with the mainland. Its use was part of a modern tradition. The first Mailboat was launched into the sea in 1876. It was a chancy way by which an isolated community could contact the mainland.

Items of mail were placed in a recess carved in the boat, a recess which was then covered by a piece of wood and made waterproof. The Mailboat was taken to the Point known as Rudh Challa, beyond the Feather Store, and placed upon the water, to be washed the 45 miles to the Hebrides and, hopefully, to be picked up and the enclosure posted to its destination.

The museum example was based on a Mailboat which was sent in 1911 to Messrs Gowans, who were woollen warehousemen in Glasgow. It was picked up at North Uist, having travelled 60 miles in about two and a-half days.

The man who initiated St. Kilda's novel Mailboat was John Sands, who apart from being imaginative had flair as a journalist. In 1870s, he conducted a series of experiments related to sending tideborne messages. The Mailboat was the best idea. It was used to advantage after a disastrous harvest in 1885. The message reached the Hebrides and action was taken to alleviate the islander's distress.

Stories of St. Kilda fascinate us because here was a people cut off from the world for most of the year. It is reported that when the first cruise boat—the paddle steamer Vulcan—visited the islands, its entry into Village Bay sent the villagers fleeing up Conachair in terror.

The St. Kildans could have maintained their self-sufficiency indefinitely without interference from tourists. Yet it was the Victorian tourists, with their love of visiting out of the way places, who would not leave St. Kilda alone. This group of islands at the edge of the world was their Ultima Thule.

Two steamers long associated with the summertime run to St. Kilda were the *Dunara Castle* and the *Hebrides*. They slid into Village Bay in the period from 1877 to 1939.

As already related, the Bay was visited by the boats of naturalists, by private yachts and by the trawlermen, especially those of Fleetwood, to whom St. Kilda—and its hake—became a special destination.

A Post Office was opened in 1900, prior to which it was felt there was no need for one. In 1877, at the start of the steamer service, the Post Office sent a Surveyor who discovered that 120 letters a year were leaving St. Kilda. Only two people, one of them being the Minister, could write. The first Postmaster, the Rev. Fiddes, received £5 a year for his pains, though for nine months of the year he had simply to store any letters until the first steamer sailing of the year took place in June.

The Postmaster from 1906 until the evacuation was Neil Ferguson, in whose term the Post Office was moved from the Factor's House to a small zinc-covered building in the Street.

The Army now handles the mail, which goes out fortnightly on the landing craft or by any visiting boat. Helicopters periodically arrive and can be used for carrying the mail. In winter, mail is dropped but cannot be collected. I had heard from a former air traffic controller at Benbecula of the mailbag lobbed from a Cessna aircraft; the bag lodged on a cliffside ledge and was recovered with difficulty.

It was Mark and one of the girls who made the Mailboats. The girl was an art student from Glasgow who was sketching on St. Kilda. The idea of communicating with the mainland by means of an engineless "boat" on the ebb tide fascinated her.

The magazine of the St. Kilda Club is called *St. Kilda Mail*. My latest copy gave examples from the 1980s of the places where Boats had been washed up—Sandoy Island, Norway, Iceland, North Uist, Lewis, Harris, and Lewis yet again. It took almost two years for the tideborne Mailboat to reach Norway.

A splendidly-posed picture in the Kearton book of 1897 showed a bearded islander wading ankle-deep and about to release a Mailboat. On the lid of the boat was the graphic message: PLEASE OPEN. Richard Kearton was so interested in the concept of the Mailboat that he persuaded a local man to make him one.

"I had it put in the sea so as to observe its behaviour, and in order that my brother might have an opportunity of photographing the man in the act of despatching it." (The photograph was not taken at the Point, unless a considerable landmass, shown in the background, has been bulldozed away).

Richard Kearton now arranged for a Mailboat to be released on March 24 in the year following his visit. It was picked up on North Uist on March 31 and the contents forwarded to him by post. The letters were readable. "Despite the fact that they had become soaked with sea water, they still

A dummy pillar box, Hirta.

retained a delightful aroma of peat smoke when they reached my hands..."

The Mailboats used by our Working Party were packed with postcards bought locally and liberally adorned with the rubber stamps signifying they were from St. Kilda, "The Furthest Station West". They were released on the ebb tide in the early evening of June 16. Two Mailboats were carefully carried down the slope to the wet rocks of the Rudh Challa. In the absence of a sheep's bladder as float and sail combined, we used large plastic containers.

The Mailboats were tossed into the water, one after another, and soon were bobbing away from the island, under the bemused stares of hungry gannets. My postcard was picked up and franked by the Post Office on June 24th. Unfortunately, I could not read the name of the village. It was delivered to my Yorkshire home on June 27. I sent a paragraph about it to the local newspaper. The sub-editor used as a heading "It's Faster by Sea..."

A letter from Ron filled in the missing detail. His card had been on the same Mailboat. Ron received a letter from the lady who found it on the beach near Miavaig on the west coast of Lewis. The lady was on a day-trip from Stornoway. "This is the second time a Mailboat of mine has been found near this same spot... The day she found it, she thought that it had just arrived as everything was bone dry. If this was so, then it took only five days to cross the Atlantic."

In the evening, I walked on to the hill where space had been marked out for the winter airdrop. The first attempts were by parachute, with the Village as the target. Usually, the chutes took their loads into the sea.

In a corner of the *Puff-inn,* the Teddy Bear and a coffin remind those in the know of an earlier effort at dropping supplies from the air. Teddy, attached to a parachute, had been hurled out to test the direction and strength of the wind. He was blown into the sea and "drowned"; when recovered, the furry aviator was given a memorable funeral.

Prospect of Village Bay.

The Village and its Bay.

Change and Decay on Hirta

MACKINNON AND MACQUEEN, Ferguson, Gillies and MacDonald—
these were the old St. Kildan families. I had got to know them well by
repute. Whenever I walked along the Street, their spirit seemed to pervade
their old haunts.

I thought especially of Finlay MacQueen, and I liked to picture him in
his early manhood. No one was more nimble on the cliffs nor more dexterous at capturing seabirds for foods.

Into my mind came an image of Finlay in later life, poring over his collection of stuffed birds or reading aloud from his Gaelic Bible before going
awa' to his bed.

I recalled the life and witness of Neil Ferguson, Postmaster, School
Manager, Elder of the Kirk, Flockmaster and much else.

I walked into the shell of what had been Cottage No.8. It was empty
at the time of the Evacuation in 1930, but here had lived "Old Blind
Callum", a thoughtful chap and one who occupied the pulpit at the kirk
when the Missionary was having a vacation on the mainland.

The Street that heard their voices, the whir and clack of the spinning
wheel and the barking of many dogs was now being kept alive by wrens
using chimneys as song perches and by the snipe "chippering" on the old
croftland.

As I strode towards Ruaival, it pleased me to imagine Hirta as it was—
to picture a young woman milking a cow, a man clipping a blackfaced

sheep and people bustling about the cleits.

Something of the communal spirit of Old Hirta is to be sensed by those who go to the kirk and see the enormous pulpit and plain pews which the islanders occupied for hours on end.

David suggested that we might gather here for a service on the Sunday, and this we did—committed Christians and agnostics alike—because it was "seemly so to do." The condition of the kirk astonished us. The building had last been used regularly almost 60 years before, but—sensitively restored by the National Trust for Scotland—the fabric was in good order, the woodwork well varnished, and all was clean and tidy.

As a prelude to the service, Ron gave a brief account of Church life on St. Kilda. David conducted the service, which began with a hymn that would certainly rouse echoes from the past: "All people that on Earth do dwell. . .''

David had written a short prayer:

> For life and health and all the good things of this life given us to use and to enjoy:
> For the beauty and wonder of your world;
> For friends, for family and for all those human relationships that can make life good;
> For this island of St. Kilda;
> For this Church
> and for the freedom to worship in it—
> We give you praise and thanks.

As a Methodist, reared on lively preaching, I had been interested, on my first visit to the kirk, to mount the steps into a pulpit that is large enough to form the bridge of a small coaster. The authorised version of The Bible lay on the rostrum, taking light from windows set behind and to one side.

Some of the girls who had been out walking returned with a story of having met a Benedictine monk who intended to hold Mass in the kirk. It was just another of the St. Kilda surprises. David and I went along to the service at the appointed time and were greeted by a monk, a most affable man who did not seem disappointed at the many empty pews; he expected there would be "just me and the angels."

We mentioned our religious allegiances, which were not Catholic, and this prompted the visitor to give brief explanations of what was happening. David rang the bell for him and two more worshippers arrived. The monk left the island by helicopter on the following day.

In the wintertimes of long ago, the faithful gathered for praise and prayer by the light given by spluttering lamps fuelled by fulmar oil. The reek must have been nauseating to off-comers.

Inscription on the gravestone of Finlay MacQueen at Kincardine-on-Forth.

When Martin Martin visited Hirta in 1697, he saw three small stone chapels. The main one, Christ's Church, which stood in what is now just a cemetery, was so small that most of the worshippers assembled in the open air. By the mid-18th century, a devout people were reported to "strictly observe the Lord's Day." When the kirk fell into disrepair, the Minister's house was used for worship.

Shortly before the service time, a man informed the St. Kildans of impending devotions with what a visitor described as "a piercing howl he had borrowed from some of the seals which frequent the neighbouring rocks." In due course, a bell was used to summon the worshippers. (It was a former ship's bell, on a wooden frame, that we rang at the start of our service).

Writers about St. Kilda have made much of a stultifying effect that church attendance had on the people; of how they spent far too much time here and neglected the vital seasonal tasks; of the fundamentalist zeal of some—and especially one—of the Ministers. Worship on St. Kilda would be no more demanding, no more protracted, no more intense than that being practised on Lewis and Harris, where they still take religion seriously.

The St. Kildan way of life began to change radically with the arrival of the tourist steamers, bearing affluent visitors, and when tales told by young folk who had been to the mainland made life on the islands at the edge o' the world seemed dull. Glasgow would be an exciting place for a lad from Hirta.

Early this century, the island women were making goods such as tweed for sale to visitors, who—coming from a materialistic society—were inclined to take advantage of them. One well-known story tells of an old woman who was given an orange in exchange for a bolt of cloth. When tins of food were being brought to Hirta, there was less inclination for the men to go and get the usual food—seabirds.

The population had its numerical ups and downs—"down" in the 18th century through smallpox; "down" in the 19th century through emigration (some booking passages to Australia) and "down" through a heavy child mortality from tetanus.

The 1914-18 war had a profound effect on Hirta. A German submarine arrived and lobbed about 70 shells towards the wireless masts that had kept the British naval authorities aware of passing traffic. The signal station was put out of action (and brought back into use a few hours later). Shells struck the Church, the Feather Store, the Factor's House and two of the cottages. A lamb was seriously injured and had to be destroyed. The submarine itself was sunk near the Flannan Islands when it returned to the scene of an earlier crime.

The winter of 1929-30 was so severe and prolonged that the Missionary wrote to the Prime Minster (a Scotsman, Ramsay MacDonald). "We are now twelve weeks without news or relief supplies. For weeks all of us have been without sugar or potatoes. Paraffin Oil is running short when we must require it for light to work our looms in the making of Highland Tweed."

Then, in January, Mary Gillies was ill with appendicitis. A visiting trawler managed to get a message to the mainland requesting medical aid. On February 15, the Fishery cruiser *Norma,* with Captain Wright on the bridge, set off for St. Kilda. She carried two doctors to attend to Mary and 23 bags of mail for the islanders.

The boat sailed from the east coast round the top of Scotland and met some angry seas in the west. An improvement in the weather was noted as she approached Hirta. A blast from the siren alerted the St. Kildans and brought a Gaelic service at the kirk to an abrupt close. The doctors were rowed ashore.

Mary Gillies, her husband and a doctor, were conveyed to the *Norma* in the island boat; the *Norma* steamed hard for Oban, arriving at 10 a.m. on the following morning. The noon train was used to convey the patient and her helpers to Glasgow. Poor Mary died.

Men with a simple white deal coffin made for an interment on St. Kilda, 1930.

When news reached St. Kilda, a weary people felt that the old way of life was no longer possible. Of the 38 who remained, only 13 were men, scarcely enough men to provide a crew for the boats and to attend to the fowling tradition that provided the islanders with much of their winter food.

No crops were planted that year.

On May 10, the islanders sent a petition to the Secretary of State as follows: "We the undersigned the Natives of St. Kilda hereby respectfully pray and petition His Majesty's Government to assist us all to leave the island this year and to find homes and occupations for us on the mainland..."

It was a great story for the Press. "Our Special Correspondent" chatted with the bearded patriarchs of Hirta—with Finlay Gillies and Finlay Mac-Queen. Headlines like "Men Wait and Women Weep" wetted the appetites of newspaper readers for stories of human interest. The young folk were anxious to turn their backs on St. Kilda. The hill track to Gleann Mor, where the cattle were summered, to be milked by the lasses, had become too steep and dreary. To the young men, the bird-haunted cliffs had lost their charm.

Readers of *The Oban Times* were told about the common Hebridean custom of taking "nips" from the ears of the sheep to indicate ownership. "One owner's sheep have three nips from the right ear... Others cut the ear elongated and brought sharply to a point. In every case, the market is different, and so the shepherds of Hirta know their own flocks.''

Finlay MacQueen, with tears in his eyes, showed the correspondent a large case of partly stuffed birds—shearwater, fulmar, guillemot, razorbill, puffin, gannet, great black-backed gull and others—which he intended to take to his new home.

''Finlay was the greatest cliffman in his day and the friend of many eminent naturalists like Seton Gordon and Cherry Kearton. Finlay is taking it perhaps hardest of all. They cannot remain alone, these old folk, who have known no other home, and whose philosophy is still the philosophy that bred our simple, God-fearing ancestors. May God keep them unsullied and unspoiled in their new surroundings.''

In August, 1930, links between the mainland and St. Kilda were systematically snipped. The *Dunara Castle* brought 666 sheep to Oban on the 6th. The work was co-ordinated by two shepherds, D. Clark and D.A. MacLaren, from Messrs Corson, of Oban auction mart. Some of the sheep were penned in the field before the Manse to await the arrival of the steamer.

Transporting sheep to the waiting steamer. A photograph from ''The Oban Times'' of 1930.

The living room of House No. 3 as it was seen by Robert Atkinson in 1930.

With livestock on board, the *Dunara Castle* made a record trip. Leaving Village Bay at 7.15 a.m., it reached Oban at 10.10 p.m. A writer in *The Oban Times* noted: "It is seldom that Oban and St. Kilda have been both seen in the daylight of one day."

Readers of that newspaper heard more about the St. Kilda sheep; they had ways of their own and did not take kindly to the attention of the collies brought from the mainland. The sheep did not seem to understand why they should leave the island; a good deal of force was used to get them down the slips and into the boats, thence to the steamer in the Bay. The work was carried out in the dark, "which did not make it easier for shepherd or sheep."

On August 26, the English fishing cruiser *Harebell*, which had been chartered for the Evacuation, arrived in Oban Bay and left for St Kilda at 6 p.m. on the following day. On the 27th, the *Dunara Castle* was back at St. Kilda, and the work of conveying the livestock and household goods on board the steamer began in the afternoon, continuing until nearly midnight.

More sheep remained on St. Kilda. The government sent three shepherds from Lewis to help with the round-up. The majority were in the steamer when it left for Oban at noon on August 28. The islanders now had the sad task of saying farewell to their homes. They drowned the dogs in the sea. The cats were left alive; it was hoped they would thrive on the St. Kilda mice.

At 6 a.m., on August 29, *HMS Harebell* took the islanders to their new homes on the mainland. In each cottage was left an open Bible and a small pile of oats. Doors were locked.

The *Dunara Castle* discharged 573 sheep and 13 cattle, also household effects, at Oban. The *Harebell* followed, arriving at Lochaline, Morvern, at 6.30 p.m. on August 29. Here she was met by the *Princess Louise* carrying furniture and other effects from Oban.

Eight of the 10 families were disembarked at Lochaline, and on landing at the pier they were received with cheers by the people of the village. So the St. Kildans were driven to their new houses on the Ardtornish estate.

The remaining two families were conveyed by the *Harebell* to Oban. A huge crowd watched the vessel arrive and the St. Kildans disembarked from its pinnace at about 8.30 p.m. The first person ashore was Neil Ferguson, the Postmaster. He met an official of the Oban Post Office to

"The Mart" Hotel at Oban where some of the St. Kildans were taken on arrival in Argyll.

enact official business. The rest of the party were conveyed to the *Mart Hotel*. This party included the Ferguson's son and daughter-in-law, also Finlay MacQueen, Mr John MacDonald, Mrs Gillies and her daughter.

From what we know of the sad experiences of St. Kildans on the mainland—and this was not the Promised Land they imagined—it is ironical that within 10 years of the Evacuation, the island had regained its military importance as the central feature of a training area for flight crews. And less than 30 years from the Evacuation, the government had acquired land for a base from which to track rockets which it was proposed to launch from the Hebrides.

St. Kilda is now a busy place, with much coming and going of military personnel, of naturalists, yachtsmen, tourists on cruise ships and working parties of the National Trust for Scotland.

All appear to catch the incurable disease known as St. Kilditis. Or, as Ron was fond of saying: "When you've been to St. Kilda, nothing is the same again."

I met a Devonian in the museum. He was round faced, blonde-haired and spoke with the rolling accent of the West Country. His birthplace could not have been much farther from St. Kilda in the context of Britain, yet he was already fascinated by the St. Kildans and their tiny world.

He wandered off down the Street. If the spirit of St. Kilda Past—of the long-dead MacKinnons and MacQueens, Fergusons, Gillies and MacDonalds—still broods over that hauntingly attractive village, then they must have marvelled at the sight of this young Saxon from Wessex who worked at one of those strange radomes on the top of the hill. . .

Above: MV *"Monaco"* bathed in rich sunlight. *Below:* Village Bay, Hirta, with a Gemini being used for transporting people and their possessions.

Homeward Bound

WE LEFT St. Kilda without fuss and without tears. There was no time to shed them. The luggage must be stowed below decks. By the time I could look round, St. Kilda was just a faint mark against a bank of mist.

MV Monaco had slipped into Village Bay unobserved. The sea-mist was dense, though inland the sun—like a gigantic blow-lamp—was burning through the cloying vapour.

The air was calm. Martin Martin had written: "If the Waves in the Bay make a Noise as they break before their beating upon the Shoar, it is an infallible Forerunner of a W. Wind; if a Black Cloud appears above the South side of the Bay, a S. Wind follows some hours afterwards. It is observed of the Sea betwixt St. Kilda and the Isles Lewis, Harries, &c. that it rages more with a N. Wind, than when it blows from any other Quarter . . ."

A Fleetwood man mentioned his one and only voyage in a local trawler. He was 11 years old. A gale began to blow; they ran for shelter in Village Bay. "I could hear a roaring sound. It was just as though a giant had been sitting at a monster organ, holding one finger on one low note. The skipper told me it was the wind roaring over Kildas."

At 11.45, a blast from the *Monaco* alerted us to her presence in the Bay. I did not actually see her until the Gemini inflatable that was being used to transport people and goods was half way to where she was lying. The mist had begun to clear, yet boats were rendered as grey blotches rather than objects with fine detail. It was reminiscent of some Japanese prints I had seen.

The weather was hazy, presaging a hot day, when Robert Atkinson left St. Kilda after his visit in 1938. "We carted all our gear down to the jetty and sat about. It was like waiting for a train. Neil (Ferguson) had sighted the ship early on but had lost her in haze. She showed only a few minutes before she blew.

"The St. Kildans were in their Sunday clothes, though Finlay [MacQueen] had a floppy white shirt and his ribboned Balmoral; he looked the professor on holiday . . . *Hebrides* soon left the islands in a thick greyish haze through which the sun struck with power diminished to cast only a faintest shadow."

We left St. Kilda at 12.45 p.m. The islands were quickly lost to sight in the mist. After four hours, conditions cleared. We cruised in a techni-coloured world. The ocean was breaking its back on the long line of the Hebridean cliffs.

The passage across the Minch was marked by a splendid sundown, with the orange-red orb flecking the wake of the ship with gold.

I went to bed at 10.30. The *Monaco* tied up against the jetty at Canna after midnight. Some of our party actually went ashore; they walked and paddled by moonlight. They did not emerge from their cabins till mid-morning.

Meanwhile, I had the foredeck of the *Monaco* to myself as she sailed by Rum, with views of Eigg and Muck, and as she voyaged by Ardnamurchan into the Sound of Mull.

It was Scotland at its most glorious.

At anchor in Oban Bay.

A great skua diving on an intruder, Hirta.

Acknowledging...

...the inspiration provided by the Kearton brothers, Richard and Cherry, who through their writing and photography first made me aware of the "islands at the edge of the world".

...the delight of knowing Frank and Betty Lowe, who voyaged from Stornoway to St. Kilda in the summer of 1929 and left me notes, photographs, a door lock and a puffin snare, as souvenirs of that visit.

...the enthusiasm of the fisherfolk of Fleetwood when telling me stories of St. Kilda as seen from the heaving decks of trawlers, and especially for the interest shown by Alice Shawcross, Peter Snasdell and Jack Kelly, who allowed me to tape their memories. (Transcripts are now in the archives of the School of Scottish Studies).

...the friendship of Jean and Kurt Reinsch, of Grassington, long-time sufferers of St. Kilditis, who nurtured my love for the islands through the long years when I was not in a position to take off enough time from Editorship to visit them.

...the faith of The National Trust for Scotland in allowing me to join a working party though I had written, under qualifications, "None—but willing!"

...the companionship of the NTS working party, led by Ron Hardie.

...the enthusiastic response from Howard Bennett when I suggested this book might appear with an "Oban Times" imprint.

...the kindness of Mary Harman, an authority on St. Kilda, who read through the text and made some helpful comments.

...the generosity of Robert Atkinson in allowing me to quote from and use pictures from his great book "Island Going".

...the support of my wife, who showed considerable understanding of my St. Kilditis and will hopefully be tolerant if I try to join another working party.